Climate Action for Busy People

Climate Action
for Busy People

Cate Mingoya-LaFortune

ISLANDPRESS | Washington | Covelo

Library of Congress Control Number: 2023951879

All Island Press books are printed on environmentally responsible materials.

Manufactured in the United States of America
10 9 8 7 6 5 4 3 2 1

Keywords: adopt a drain, adopt a tree, asphalt, climate activism, climate change, climate justice, climate resilience, climate safe neighborhoods, coalition building, Depave.org, environmental justice, extreme heat, extreme weather, flooding, green infrastructure, Groundwork USA, HOLC, municipal government, parking lots, permeable surfaces, redlining, storm drains, systems change, tree equity, tree planting, urban forestry, urban heat island, zoning

To my mother, who would have liked this.
And to June, who sees with such clarity and with whom I very much like to do this work.

Contents

Introduction

THIS BOOK IS FOR ANYONE who has a case of the "climate bubble guts," the churning anxiety that comes from considering the climate crisis and the threat that it poses to us all. Each day we come across stories about the greenhouse effect, plummeting biodiversity, floods, fires, and extreme heat—it's no wonder your blood pressure is up and your stomach is grinding! The United States has lived with the knowledge of pollution and a changing climate for generations, but the solutions we've been given, especially since the end of the last century, don't come close to making a dent in what is a true global emergency. Recycle! Cut the plastic rings from your soda cans! Line dry your laundry! While these are all things you should try to do, they tend to feel minor and divorced from the day-to-day reality of rising seas and forest fires. There's an uncomfortable gap between the enormity of the problem and the perception of what the average person can do about it.

For just as long as we've known about the threats to our planet, major polluters have worked overtime to convince the average person that when it comes to the climate crisis, nothing *can* be done, nothing *should* be done, or all this is *your* fault because you took that road trip last summer and don't thoroughly wash your recyclables. While it's true that individuals have an important role to play in reducing our global carbon footprint, and thus our overall climate risk, that responsibility is even greater for corporations, utility providers, and all levels of government. The reality is that while there is increasing recognition of, and investment from the public and private sectors in, climate mitigation and adaptation, that change is still going to take years—maybe even decades—to be realized, if it happens at all. In the meantime, we're stuck with flooding streets and summer days so hot that they're literally melting transportation infrastructure.

Regulation and legislative change are both necessary, but that work is by its nature slow going, complicated, and without easy entry points for the average person to meaningfully participate. And even if we *were* able to successfully enact sweeping regulation to stop all emissions this very minute, a century of ever-rising greenhouse gas emissions has locked our planet into a certain level of screwed that we must adapt to if we want to save lives and ensure that everyone has the opportunity to live in healthy and safe spaces.

I write this book as someone who is concerned about a livable future. I also write as a longtime resident of environmental justice communities, a former teacher, and a current climate adaptation and land use professional working to improve the resilience of places threatened by the climate crisis. The people I've met in my sixteen years of people-centered community work are ready to adapt their neighborhoods to the realities of a warming planet but feel unprepared or as though they don't have the time or expertise to make a difference. We've all got rent to make, bills to pay, and laundry to do, and not all of us can or want to make a living battling the climate crisis. We can, though, take a few quick and simple steps toward making a meaningful difference.

In my role, I've helped communities across the states make changes to the built environment, to the way resources are distributed at the municipal level, and to how residents come together to effect change and pursue justice. Throughout this book, you'll see me mention Groundwork, a national network of grassroots, people-centered, environmental justice nonprofits that work on issues of climate adaptation, land reuse, and youth empowerment. My work with Groundwork USA building out the Climate Safe Neighborhoods partnership, as well as organizing I've done in my own communities, has introduced me to a balm for climate anxiety: the equity-focused, people-centered adaptation solutions already underway in communities across the country. From Richmond, California, to Richmond, Virginia, and everywhere in between, wise, lasting, stable change is happening, and I'm excited to bring the methods and lessons learned here to you.

This book offers a new perspective on how to channel the resources you currently have, big and small, to effect meaningful change at the local level that will prepare and strengthen your community against the most common climate-related challenges. The changes that must be made to keep your town's commercial district walkable, your cooling bills manageable, your air breathable, and your basements dry are ones best accomplished at the local level: where you live and by the people who live there. Working to devise and implement solutions with those closest to the effects of the climate crisis leads to smarter and more stable outcomes because they directly respond to lived experience. Local action allows us to build community and helps us to lean into our human responsibility to one another, share the work, and keep one another safe as things get weird. And things are already pretty weird.

Here in eastern Massachusetts, we spent a recent July under a pink and orange sun, cloaked in stagnant wildfire smoke blown clear across the continent from Oregon and western Canada. After a few days, wind and rainstorms cleared the haze, but, as it had for much of the spring, the rain kept coming … and coming. While some friends and neighbors complained of puddles in their basements and water-logged gardens, others complained about the unusually high heat. We'd had eleven humid days above 90°F before the first of July, with many more to come—almost unheard of in Boston, which is better known for its blizzards than its blistering heat. That same summer, Hurricane Ida swept up the eastern seaboard, pausing in New England long enough to drop tornadoes along Cape Cod, leaving unprepared residents to shelter in closets and bathtubs. Soon after, a months-long drought settled in, yellowing the grass, withering flowers and trees, and leaving the clay-heavy soil as hard and impermeable as cement—and thus incapable of absorbing rainwater, which then flowed back into basements during the next storm. While none of these individual weather events is a promise of exactly what is to come, they sound the alarm that things are changing and that it is time to prepare for a world much different than what we have known before.

So, what can we do?

First, we can let go of the idea that there's a single 100 percent—or even 10 percent—solution that is going to fix things. That solution doesn't exist. There's no panacea, no action that's going to solve centuries of environmental, economic, and racial injustice or keep everyone from Bangor, Maine, to San Diego, California, safe from the climate crisis. Instead, what we can do is bring together enough manageable, hyperlocal solutions to tip the scales in our favor before many of these extreme weather events hit the ground.

Second, we can look to success at the local level. While the next decade will bring state and federal resources for climate adaptation, there are limits as to how much a policy maker in Washington, DC, knows about the day-to-day experience of heat for a family in Miami, Florida, or how to make flooding more manageable in Milwaukee, Wisconsin. However, from coast to coast, individuals, small organizations, and community groups are taking the reins and driving their neighborhoods toward a more livable future by making changes to their built environment, their social connections, and the distribution of municipal resources.

Third, we can take stock of the resources we *do* have—time, money, relationships, knowledge, curiosity—and apply them to influencing the decisions that are made in our cities and towns. The threats to our communities are real, and feelings of fear often come linked to a perception of scarcity. Pushing back against the climate crisis will require recognizing that we have an abundance of resources at our disposal that can be used to make real, lasting change—we just need to know where to look for them and how to leverage them. With a relentless flow of stories about record heat waves, deadly landslides, and powerful hurricanes, it can feel as though there is no point in acting—that we're just a decade or two away from a *Mad Max*–style climate dystopia. Take a few deep breaths and calm your limbic system because we already have plenty of examples of neighborhoods in the United States that are well prepared for the climate crisis: neighborhoods with dense tree canopies, natural water capture systems, thoughtfully planned greenspaces, and clever community cooling infrastructure. Our current challenge is that these adaptation measures are disproportionately clustered in a few very wealthy areas. That same infrastructure that clears and cools the air in the wealthy part of town needs to be available to everyone. From "adopt-a-storm-drain" programs to depaving parties, microforests to solar benches, rain gardens to rain barrels, there are dozens of relatively easy ways your community can reduce the risk it faces from the climate crisis. Some adaptation measures can get off the ground in just a Saturday afternoon alone or with the help of a handful of neighbors; others will require long-term consensus building and commitments from your municipal government.

The interventions in this book are aimed at people living and working in communities directly impacted by climate change—those whose neighborhoods do not have adequate tree coverage or whose homes flood regularly or become dangerously hot. It is also for folks who want to help make *all* parts of their city safer, not just where they live. Regardless of your experience or expertise, it is possible to achieve tangible, meaningful changes with just a handful of hours stolen from nights and weekends. And I promise that it's worth the investment.

As you move through this book, it's important to keep a few things in mind. When you're working on issues that directly impact you, you're the expert. As you seek to help others, though, be sure to connect with those who are most impacted and prioritize their voices and expertise. A large part of climate justice work is fixing the harm caused by the environmental and structural racism and classism that have shaped our built environments. You can help. You can lead in *your* community, and you can lend your attention, your time, your knowledge, and your resources to *others*. Effecting change at the systems level requires you to build a coalition of the right people, an understanding of the change that's required to repair the existing harm and prevent that harm from happening again, and a clear-eyed view of the barriers to that change.

I'm not going to tell you to write to your congressperson or pressure you to buy an electric car. I'm not going to admonish you for flying to see your family or getting an iced coffee in a plastic cup. What I will do is help you understand exactly why you and your neighbors are experiencing risks from the climate crisis and walk you through the small steps you can take, right now, to make change where you live. Throughout this book, I share my professional experiences in community-based and climate-focused action and organizing, as well as my personal experience effecting change in the communities I've lived in. Many of the ideas presented here are drawn from successful real-life examples that have helped communities make their neighborhoods climate resilient and are also transferable to communities that are dealing with other challenges around issues like transportation, housing, and education.

This book is roughly divided into three parts. The first section helps us understand why our communities look the way they do (spoiler: it's not by accident!) and digs into the most pressing climate risks facing cities and towns. The second section digs into what you can do right now, today, this very minute, alone or with a small group of friends, to keep your community or one you care about safer from the climate crisis. The third section focuses on how to build effective coalitions to change how decisions are made and resources are distributed at the local level.

We've known about the threats of the climate crisis for over a century, and although the federal and state levels of government have failed to pass and enforce the statues and regulations necessary to secure a safe and equitable future, all is not lost. One of the biggest threats we face is within our control: it's the threat of losing hope, of thinking that no change is possible under the current system. This moment of crisis calls on us to push past that despair in the name of ourselves, our ancestors, and future generations.

We are all capable of effecting some type of change, of leveraging existing ideas and resources into meaningful local transformations. So, if you're ready to kick off your first small, local solution, turn the page and let's get started!

CHAPTER 1

It's No Accident

THE NEIGHBORHOOD I GREW UP IN WAS A JOY. In the summer, the boys settled onto the front stoop to get their hair buzzed, while the girls' beaded braids clicked and clacked away through endless rounds of Double Dutch. Like the other kids, I loved to sit in the shade of the only tree on our sidewalk—a small but sturdy maple planted by the city in the early 1980s. And like the other kids, I spent a lot of time in and out of the hospital for asthma triggered by the exhaust coming from the nearby expressway and the mildewing walls of our frequently flooded basements. On the other side of the road, set a few blocks back from the zipping cars and diesel trucks, was a much different neighborhood. There, the yards were blanketed with grass and flowers, and mature trees stretched past the row house roof lines, casting a refreshing shade that cut through the heat. Unpaved yards with bushes and trees soaked up rainwater before it had a chance to seep through basement walls.

We know that the climate crisis is making our weather hotter, wetter, and more unpredictable, but because of the way resources are distributed in the United States, people don't experience the consequences of a warming planet equally from state to state, from city to city within the same state, or even from neighborhood to neighborhood—or block to block—within the same city. And that's not by accident. The differences between my childhood neighborhood and the one across the expressway are repeated almost identically across the country, and those differences all have an origin story.

Figure 1-1 shows a Google Earth image of the Lower Price Hill neighborhood in Cincinnati, Ohio. On a hot and sunny day, you, like me, would probably want to hang out on the left side of the black dashed line. There, a dense and lush tree canopy cover casts shade over the sidewalks and apartments of a residential neighborhood, making a hot July day a bit more bearable. The majority of the roofs are white or light gray, reflecting back the sun's light and lowering the buildings' cooling costs. Grassy yards and the root systems of mature trees absorb rainwater, keeping it out of basements and from overwhelming the city's sewer system and streets. On the right side, which, I can't emphasize enough, is *on the same block* as the left side of this image, the picture is much different. Dead and desiccated tree trunks punctuate a sparse and scrawny canopy. Scraggly shrubs fail to cast shade or keep up with the heat radiating off of the ocean of concrete, asphalt, and black rubber roofs. With fewer plants or patches of soil to soak up the rain, the right side is more likely to flood than the left side.

If you zoom out from this image and look at the maps of Cincinnati shown in figures 1-2 and 1-3, specifically the Lower Price Hill neighborhood outlined in black, what you see up close in the photograph is amplified across the entire city. In figure 1-2, the

Figure 1-1: Aerial view of the Lower Price Hill neighborhood in Cincinnati, Ohio, looking north. The right side of the gray line has more impermeable pavement and fewer trees, adding to the urban heat island effect. (Map data: Google Earth © 2023 Landsat/Copernicus.)

dark shading shows where a dense tree canopy covers the north and northwest sections of the city, whereas in the southeast corner of the city there is sparse shade; there you're more likely to find a large parking lot than a park. That patchy tree cover east of Lower Price Hill has a significant impact on the way residents experience heat. Figure 1-3 shows the air temperature in Cincinnati, which considers both the heat and humidity. Areas with a tree canopy are significantly cooler throughout the day and night than areas without.

Although the maps shown are from Cincinnati, Ohio, this juxtaposition can easily be found in cities and towns from Delaware to California. Areas that are shaded, cool, and dry sit just blocks away from their hot, wet, smoggy neighbors. It's easy to look at the

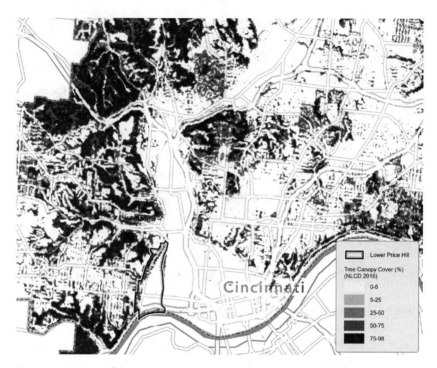

Figure 1-2: Map of the tree canopy cover in Cincinnati, Ohio. The tree canopy cover in the northwestern part of the city is much denser than in the south-eastern portion of the city. (Data source: National Land Cover Database 2016. Map by Lawrence Hoffman.)

layout of a municipality and conclude that what you're seeing—the types of buildings, the placement of asphalt, the route of a rail line—were all placed organically over time. It might seem that as one plot of land was filled, developers just moved on to the next. It's easy to think the same about where people live. When we talk about historically ethnic neighborhoods, such as Little Italy, Chinatown, or Little Haiti, the dominant narrative goes that as people migrated to the United States, they settled where their friends and family members settled. It's true that people live near others who are like them in terms of class, cultural identity, or values, but

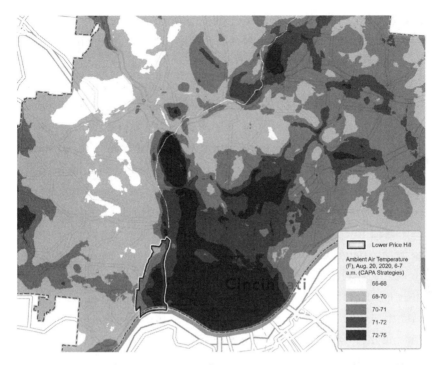

Figure 1-3: Map of early morning ambient air temperature in Cincinnati, Ohio. The areas with fewer trees stay much hotter throughout the night and into the early morning than areas with more trees. (Data source: CAPA Strategies Heat Watch—Cincinnati, Ohio, 2020. Map by Lawrence Hoffman.)

why did groups settle on the specific land they settled on? And why for so long? The details may look different from community to community, but everything from the size of a building to its inhabitants has a history vital to understanding the threat posed by climate change.

There is a direct connection between how local and federal city planning and housing policies shaped both the built environment and the modern climate crisis in the United States. From the 1930s through the 1970s, race-based housing segregation, urban renewal, the development of the federal highway system, and many other programs intended to improve the lives of certain Americans had disastrous effects on low-income communities and communities of color who, at the time, lacked the social capital and political representation to effectively push back.[1] For example, let's look at the process known as "redlining." Most homeowners today have a twenty- or thirty-year federally backed mortgage that allows them to spread a large amount of debt over a long period of time at a stable interest rate. Homeownership would be a lot more challenging without this tool if, instead of spreading out the cost of a $400,000 home over twenty or thirty years, you were expected to come up with the money in just five years or be forced to remortgage at what could be a much higher interest rate. In the early twentieth century, the mortgages Americans enjoy today didn't exist. Instead, banks offered home loans in five-year increments. At the end of the five years, if the mortgage wasn't paid off, the balance would have to be remortgaged at whatever rates were prevalent at the time.

This system chugged along until the Great Depression hit and the United States was staring down a serious foreclosure crisis. By 1933, nearly 50 percent of mortgages were in default, thousands of small and large banks and lending institutions had shut their doors, and over a quarter of Americans were out of work. To keep families in their homes and loosen lending from private banks, the Franklin D. Roosevelt administration launched the federally backed mortgage as part of a New Deal package of economic and social programs. The federally backed mortgage, which is still available today, pledges to private lenders that the government will vouch for certain borrowers and cover the full cost of their loan defaults using taxpayer funding.

To figure out which loans were eligible to be insured by the government, the federal Home Owners' Loan Corporation (HOLC)

contracted with surveyors across the country to develop "risk assessment maps."[2] These maps separated neighborhoods into four
categories or "grades." Those outlined in green or "greenlined"
were the most favorable and were graded "A" to signal that homes
in that area were considered a relatively safe bet for investment.
Green areas boasted high-quality housing stock, pleasant environmental conditions, and White residents. Remember that who is
considered White in American culture changes over time. If you're
of Italian, Eastern European, or Irish descent, you might be considered White today, but you would have been the "wrong kind" of
White person according to the HOLC and been prohibited from
getting federally backed home loans or would have had to pay unfavorable interest rates. On the other end of the spectrum, neighborhoods outlined in red or "redlined" were graded "D" to signal
that they were considered a highly risky investment. In between
these extreme grades were "bluelined" neighborhoods graded "B"
for still desirable and "yellowlined" neighborhoods graded "C" for
declining. Residents in yellow and redlined communities were denied federally backed mortgages or received private lending at unfavorable rates. Their homes were of lower-quality housing stock
and in closer proximity to pollutants.[3] Another deciding factor for
a C or D grade was the presence of non-White residents, specifically Black and Brown residents (D-graded areas), but also "undesirable" ethnicities such as immigrants and Jewish people (C- and
some D-graded areas). One of the most telling and unsettling parts
of the HOLC's risk assessment maps can be found in the maps'
"clarifying remarks" sections, which detail the surveyors' rationale
for grading neighborhoods as they did. These notes illustrate how
focused surveyors were on explicitly disadvantaging non-White
communities. Published in 1933, an area description regarding
a C-graded or yellowlined neighborhood in Richmond, Virginia

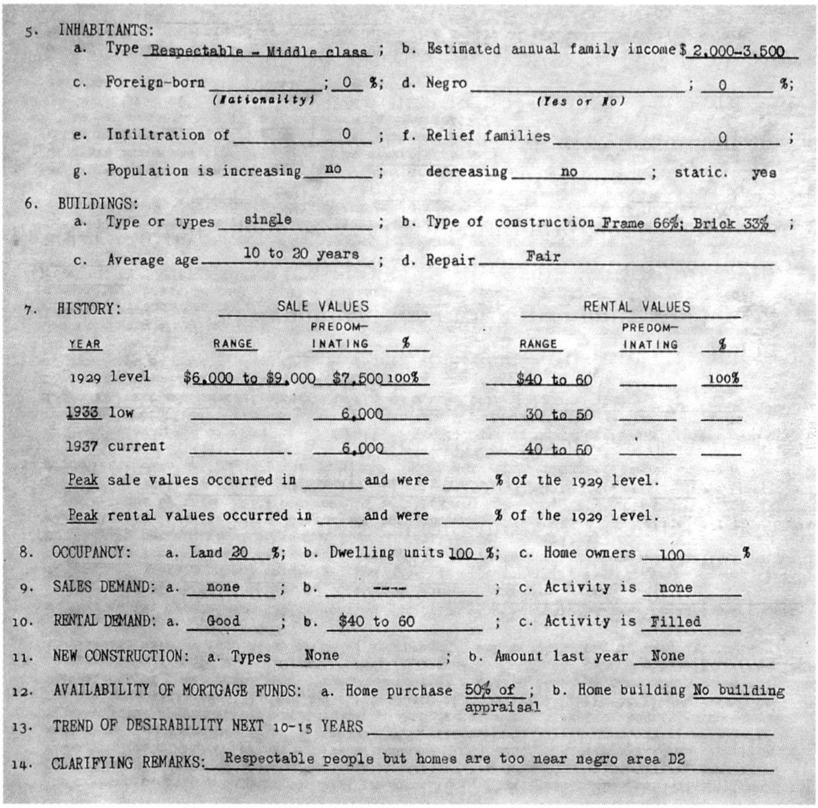

5. INHABITANTS:
a. Type Respectable - Middle class ; b. Estimated annual family income $ 2,000-3,500
c. Foreign-born ______ ; 0 %; d. Negro ______ ; 0 %;
(Nationality) (Yes or No)
e. Infiltration of 0 ; f. Relief families 0 ;
g. Population is increasing no ; decreasing no ; static. yes

6. BUILDINGS:
a. Type or types single ; b. Type of construction Frame 66%; Brick 33% ;
c. Average age 10 to 20 years ; d. Repair Fair

7. HISTORY:

YEAR	SALE VALUES RANGE	PREDOM-INATING	%	RENTAL VALUES RANGE	PREDOM-INATING	%
1929 level	$6,000 to $9,000	$7,500	100%	$40 to 60		100%
1933 low		6,000		30 to 50		
1937 current		6,000		40 to 60		

Peak sale values occurred in ____ and were ____ % of the 1929 level.
Peak rental values occurred in ____ and were ____ % of the 1929 level.

8. OCCUPANCY: a. Land 20 %; b. Dwelling units 100 %; c. Home owners 100 %
9. SALES DEMAND: a. none ; b. ---- ; c. Activity is none
10. RENTAL DEMAND: a. Good ; b. $40 to 60 ; c. Activity is Filled
11. NEW CONSTRUCTION: a. Types None ; b. Amount last year None
12. AVAILABILITY OF MORTGAGE FUNDS: a. Home purchase 50% of appraisal ; b. Home building No building
13. TREND OF DESIRABILITY NEXT 10-15 YEARS ______
14. CLARIFYING REMARKS: Respectable people but homes are too near negro area D2

Figure 1-4: Clarifying Remarks from a "C"-graded neighborhood in Richmond, Virginia. Remarks read: "Respectable people, but homes are too near negro area D2." (Redlining map of Richmond, Virginia, and Environs; April 3, 1937. National Archives at College Park, College Park, MD.)

(figure 1-4) reads, "Respectable people, but homes are too near negro area D2."[4] This quote demonstrates that the very proximity to Blackness, let alone being Black oneself, was enough to rob residents of access to the preeminent method of building intergenerational wealth in American culture: homeownership.

It's important to note that the HOLC did not cause segregation in the United States, but it did federally codify segregation that had long been legislated at the municipal level. If you owned a home in a redlined neighborhood, your home's value was depressed because prospective buyers were unable to get a federally backed mortgage to spread their debt out over twenty or thirty years using a stable interest rate. This kept residents of redlined areas from selling their homes for much of a profit or from taking out equity to make much-needed repairs and improvements. Additionally, the lower home values for residents of redlined areas meant lower contributions to the city's coffers through property taxes. These communities fell to the bottom of the list when it came time for cities to choose where to invest in parks, plant trees, and upgrade sewage infrastructure because residents lacked both sociopolitical power and the markers of wealth due to their race or ethnicity. If you were a family of color who had the money and desire to live in a bluelined or greenlined area, you were kept out by lenders, real estate brokers, and property owners fearing that the presence of "subversive racial elements" would cause their neighborhood to be downgraded.

This history still impacts communities, even though the 1968 Fair Housing Act outlawed race-based housing discrimination and the use of redlining maps to make decisions about home mortgage lending.[5] Today, about 74 percent of formerly redlined neighborhoods are still majority low to moderate income, and 64 percent are majority minority.[6] As James Baldwin once said, "History is not the past. It is the present."[7]

But this book is about the climate crisis. Why spend all this time talking about who gets to live where in our cities and towns if what we're trying to do is understand events like extreme heat or storms? The maps shown in figures 1-5 through 1-8 are of Elizabeth in New Jersey's Union County, which is just west of New York City. Figure 1-5 shows a digitization of the 1936 redlining map for

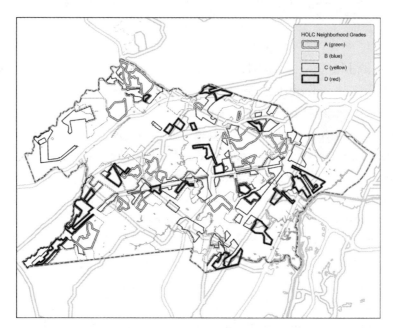

Figure 1-5: HOLC neighborhood grades for Elizabeth, New Jersey. "Greenlined" areas were eligible for federally backed mortgages; "redlined" areas were ineligible for federally backed mortgages. (Map by Lawrence Hoffman.)

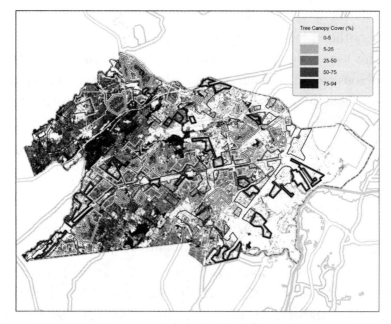

Figure 1-6: HOLC neighborhood grades for Elizabeth, New Jersey, overlaid with 2016 tree canopy cover data. Formerly redlined areas have far fewer trees than formerly greenlined areas. (Map by Lawrence Hoffman.)

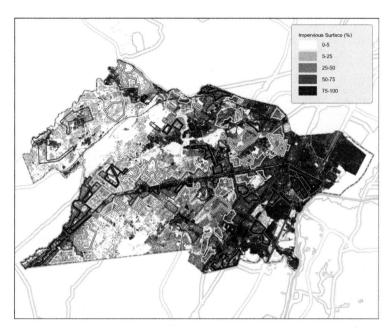

Figure 1-7: HOLC neighborhood grades for Elizabeth, New Jersey, overlaid with 2016 impervious surface data. Formerly redlined areas have more pavement than formerly greenlined areas. (Map by Lawrence Hoffman.)

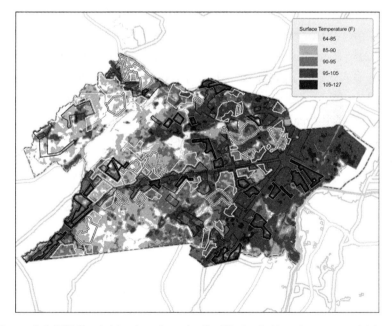

Figure 1-8: HOLC neighborhood grades for Elizabeth, New Jersey, overlaid with 2016 land surface temperature data. Formerly redlined areas are hotter than formerly greenlined areas. (Map by Lawrence Hoffman.)

Union County, New Jersey. Find any greenlined area. Remember that those areas had good housing stock, had the "right" kind of White person, and were eligible for federally backed mortgages. Find that same area in figure 1-6, which shows tree canopy cover across Union County as of 2016, and then in figure 1-7, which shows impermeable pavement such as driveways, parking lots, and roads as of 2016. Finally, find that area in figure 1-8, which shows relative heat as of 2016; the darkest areas are the hottest. Then go back to figure 1-5, find any redlined area, and track that area again through figures 1-6, 1-7, and 1-8.

What do you notice?

What you're likely observing is that formerly redlined areas have fewer trees, have more pavement, and are hotter than formerly greenlined neighborhoods. That said, it can be hard to extrapolate what this looks like at the city level just by looking at the map alone. The bar chart shown in figure 1-9 translates the data you see visualized in the maps of Elizabeth, New Jersey, into a powerful picture of the distribution of climate risk. As you go from formerly greenlined (A) to formerly redlined (D), the tree canopy cover (light gray) decreases. The impervious surfaces (dark gray), which we can use as a proxy for increased urban heat island and flood risk, increase, and the land surface temperature (black) increases. Nationwide, neighborhoods that were redlined have on average half as many trees as formerly greenlined neighborhoods, and what few trees exist are significantly smaller and lower to the ground than typical, limiting their ability to cool the surrounding environment or retain stormwater.

But wait, it gets worse. Research conducted by Jeremy Hoffman and Vivek Shandas in 2020 found that formerly redlined neighborhoods are approximately 4.5°F hotter on average than their formerly greenlined counterparts, but that difference can be as extreme as 25°F at the same time on the same summer's day.[8] The impact of that difference is substantial. It is the difference between turning your air conditioner on and not. The difference between a cooling bill you can pay at the end of July and one that you absolutely cannot afford. The difference between letting your kids play outside with their friends on a summer afternoon or keeping them indoors to prevent a heat-induced asthma attack. There are social, economic, and health consequences to how we experience the built environment. From COVID-19 deaths to kidney disease and maternal mortality to heart attacks, residents of formerly redlined neighborhoods currently experience higher risks of most diseases and chronic health conditions. The one exception to this is cancer, which is a disease one usually ages into. With life expectancy that can be up to fifteen years lower for residents of formerly redlined neighborhoods than those of formerly greenlined neighborhoods, too many die before they can reach the age where others develop cancer.[9]

Redlining is one example of how discriminatory policies and practices reverberate through the generations, but it is by no means the only one. In the post–World War II period, federally and state-funded urban renewal initiatives razed the homes, businesses, and community institutions of low-income, immigrant, and non-White communities to make way for modernized public infrastructure. The vision of new and forward-looking urban environments was constructed by overwhelmingly White middle- and upper-class engineers who never lived in such neighborhoods and summarily ignored the displacement and harm caused by urban renewal. Their vision reframed America's cities as something for the "right kind" of White people to pass through in their cars on the way to work, commercial districts, and cultural institutions. They poured mountains of state and federal resources into wealth

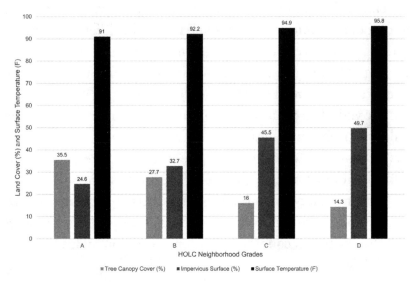

Figure 1-9: Bar chart illustrating the relationship between HOLC neighborhood grade and tree canopy cover (light gray), impervious surface (dark gray), and heat (black) in Elizabeth, New Jersey, as measured in 2016. As you move from greenlined areas (A) to redlined areas (D), communities have fewer trees, more pavement, and greater land surface temperatures. (Chart by Lawrence Hoffman.)

building for some, while the poor, immigrants, and people of color were forced to leave their homes and communities with little to no recompense. Federally sponsored White flight out of cities and into suburban communities; restrictive covenants baked into the deeds and neighborhood culture, preventing the sale or rental of property to certain individuals based on race, gender, or sexual orientation; aging infrastructure that the city can't afford to repair—there's a history to why our communities look the way they do. This isn't an accident.

In the New Orleans neighborhood of Tremé, Claiborne Avenue was once a walkable, bustling, commercial and residential district for its upper-middle-class and predominantly Black community.

Throughout the nineteenth and early twentieth centuries, a linear park ran along the middle of the avenue, and soaring hundred-year-old live oaks, dripping with Spanish moss, provided shade under which residents would play music, promenade, and socialize outdoors despite the summer heat and afternoon downpours. But by the late 1950s, Claiborne Avenue was in the crosshairs of urban renewal advocates. As part of a development plan for the federal highway system, the greenway and a significant stretch of homes were replaced by the Claiborne Avenue Expressway. Today, alongside the smog from cars and trucks, the impermeable pavement retains the sun's heat during the day and releases it through the night, contributing to New Orleans's position as the worst heat island in the United States.[10] The endless stretch of blacktop and lack of sewer drains cause stormwater to collect in the streets and flood nearby homes.

From federally backed mortgage lending to urban renewal to the siting of industry, the infrastructure decisions of local and federal governments have shaped our built environment in ways that saddle some communities with blacktop and endless smog. Meanwhile, others enjoy greenspaces and high ground.

One of the most common explanations I hear for why communities still look the way they do is that those who face racism or struggle to make ends meet are too busy and distracted to care about environmental justice issues. While it's true that those who face structural oppression are concerned with and fatigued by those barriers, the idea that they don't care about protecting their community from pollution or the climate crisis couldn't be further from the truth. In the Black neighborhood where I was raised, parents paid close attention to temperature reports and smog indices, keeping children indoors and inhalers close at hand as soon as asthma risk warnings were issued. The problems of the built

Figure 1-10 and Figure 1-11: Aerial photograph of St. Bernard Circle in New Orleans, Louisiana, in 1942 compared to a Google Earth image of the same location in October 2022. (Figure 1-10: Courtesy of The City Archives & Special Collections, New Orleans Public Library. Photo by A. E. Stewart. Figure 1-11: Google Earth © 2023 Landsat/Copernicus.)

and natural environment had real-world, tangible consequences for their children's lives. To tens of millions of others nationwide, issues of flooding, heat, ice storms, and fires are similarly tangible. Hotter summers mean higher cooling bills, which put a strain on household budgets. If a creek overflows into the basement, the resulting mold is a health hazard to the whole family. Factories, transfer stations, and bus depots have to go somewhere, but they are frequently crammed into neighborhoods of color that lack the political capital to reject them and clear their air. Black, Brown, immigrant, and low- and moderate-income communities all care deeply about the consequences of the climate crisis and environmental injustice where they live, but they often lack respect from the political and social systems that were built to intentionally exclude them from decision-making.

That's not to say that if you live in a formerly greenlined neighborhood, or one that wasn't subjected to urban renewal, your community isn't suffering or struggling from the climate crisis or doesn't require improvements. Throughout the country, almost every neighborhood is going to require interventions to address extreme weather conditions. But, just like the residents who live on that shady portion of the block in western Lower Price Hill, we're all closer and more deeply connected to an area of risk than we think.

At this point, if you're familiar with US history, you're likely deeply disappointed but not terribly surprised by any of this conversation. However, you might feel betrayed. The back cover and introduction to this book both clearly promise hope that change is possible, and now I've just laid out a depressing, systems-level, multigenerational explanation for environmental injustice, one that you had nothing to do with and one that you have very little

Figure 1-12: Vision to Reality Park in New Orleans, Louisiana. This park was built by Groundwork New Orleans as a flood and heat mitigation measure, a native plant and wildlife habitat, and a recreation space for those living and walking along Claiborne Avenue. (Photo by author.)

individual control over. I'm sorry. That was all objectively a bummer to read, but I promise I had a good reason for bringing it all up.

The history, policy, and leadership behind land use decisions matter. We're not just looking to stop the harm caused by historical and contemporary decisions; we're looking to keep that harm from happening again. We have to know where to look for risk and where to intervene. Part of doing this work is understanding that our neighborhoods don't look the way they do by accident and, importantly, that they won't change by accident. It's going to take a deliberate, thoughtful approach to identify the small 1 percent solutions that can make a difference and to keep an eye out for the policies and decisions that, like the highways built during urban renewal, may promise progress but instead bring harm. Know that you're not alone in wrestling with this knowledge and in doing this work. Individuals and groups are already out there, making these changes to policy and the built environment.

Along a section of the Claiborne Ave expressway, Groundwork New Orleans, a local environmental justice and workforce development nonprofit, has built Vision to Reality Park (figure 1-12), a greenspace equipped with benches to rest upon, shade structures to protect visitors from the heat, and a stunning bioswale packed with native pollinators that captures, cleans, and diverts stormwater from the surrounding residential neighborhood. Although the park does not eliminate or repair the long-standing harm from the social and cultural impacts of the past, it reduces a very real harm that is happening right now by cooling and cleaning the air and reducing flooding. This park was designed and built by local New Orleanians living in neighborhoods impacted by the climate crisis—residents who are intimately familiar with the land, water, and its challenges, and who have a vision for the future of their community. Small projects like Vision to Reality Park show us that the built environment can be changed in ways that give us time and space to figure out what's next.

CHAPTER 2

Hot, Wet, and Smoky

BEFORE I MOVED INTO THE CLIMATE ADAPTATION SPACE, I taught middle school science. Ask any teacher: the first few weeks of school are equally exciting and exhausting for both kids and adults as everyone learns new names and routines. In my classroom, the beginning of the school year was marked by sweat. Our hundred-year-old building was located in the densest concentration of public housing in the United States, set a few blocks from a metal scrap yard and just off a major cross-borough parkway. Due to the age of the building, there was no centralized cooling system, and due to tight budgets, not all classrooms had functioning window air-conditioning units. As the mercury rose, I relied on one large workhorse of an industrial fan parked in the corner to cool myself and more than thirty tweens. At the end of class, I'd collect my students' assignments and find the packets wet and rippled where sweat had dripped from the children's faces to the paper below.

Outdoor recess offered almost no relief from the heat, especially as the afternoon crept on. With no shade structures or trees in or around the play yard, the blacktop soaked up the September sun, giving the space the feeling of a convection oven. A handful of kids would push through the heat, intent on a basketball rematch or to show off their new dance moves, but for the most part, students and teachers would crowd together, sluggish and dripping with sweat, under the narrow band of shadow cast by the building itself. On hot days, more inhalers came out to ease the breathing of the many children with asthma, and those who didn't get a chance to burn off their energy through a game of tag or a dance battle because of the heat struggled to focus in class.

These challenges are only becoming more intense and widespread as climate change exacerbates risks like heat, flooding, and fire. Across the country, school districts have had to shorten school days or weeks because of dangerous heat waves. During my first summer in eastern Massachusetts, a heat wave canceled the first week of school for more than twenty districts.[1] Without air conditioning, school administrators felt unable to provide a safe learning environment for children as outdoor temps crept toward 100°F. Years—and multiple heat waves—later, summer weather seems to have permanently extended into the beginning and end of the school year, and some communities are adapting to keep kids safe and learning. School districts in Los Angeles are exploring ways to build greenspaces on campuses to add shade and relief from scorching pavement, and schools in Ohio are exploring options for adding cooling systems to old buildings.[2] The climate issues that school districts are facing are the same ones impacting neighborhoods across the United States more broadly. Recognizing major climate risks to your community can help you identify how and where to intervene.

Heat

The climate crisis is making excessive heat events more severe and more frequent, exacerbating the associated dangers. Heat kills more people in the United States than most of the other natural disasters—floods, hurricanes, blizzards, and earthquakes combined—and experts believe the number of deaths from heat is likely underreported.[3] Increased temperatures impact human health and safety, triggering preterm births, heart attacks, respiratory issues, and mental health disorders. Vulnerable populations, such as young children, the elderly, and the economically disadvantaged, are at higher risk when the temperatures rise because of how excessive heat affects human health and because they have less control over keeping themselves cool, but even the young and the healthy can unexpectedly fall ill from small increases in temperature. As our cities and towns get warmer, we face an urgent threat that quietly sneaks up on us from one summer to the next.

During the first year of Groundwork USA's Climate Safe Neighborhoods partnership, we led door-knocking campaigns in five cities, talking to residents about their experiences with summer temperatures. Across the board, residents were, at first blush, unconcerned with heat, especially in the South. "It's summer! Of course it's warm," we'd hear, or "I've lived here all my life, and it's always hot." However, when we dug deeper, we found that residents have subtly changed their behavior and financial expenditures because of rising temperatures. In Richmond, Virginia, a community elder informed organizers that she no longer chats with her neighbors for much of the summer because it is too warm to sit on her porch. She has a heart condition that is exacerbated by the heat. In Pawtucket, Rhode Island, a woman spoke about how, when she first got her dog, she'd take him for a walk on her lunch break at noon. Now, by midday, the sidewalk burns her dog's paws, and she's had to adjust her schedule to walk him at either 10 a.m. or after work. A resident of the Elizabethport neighborhood in Elizabeth, New Jersey, noted how hesitant he was to run his window-unit air conditioners because electricity is expensive and that bill at the end of the month can mean going without his medication. The heat, even in places familiar with hot weather, is changing the way we spend money, connect with our communities, and organize our lives.

Urban areas experience hotter temperatures and more pro-longed heat thanks to the "urban heat island effect," a phenom-enon whereby solar radiation is absorbed by structures such as rooftops and asphalt that then radiate the energy back out. Natural landscapes, such as trees, bodies of water, and vegetation, absorb less heat than nonporous surfaces, such as sidewalks and park-ing lots. Cities are prone to becoming heat islands because they usually contain more built structures and fewer greenspaces than nonurban areas. While the air temperature—the number on the thermometer—might read the same across a city, the urban heat island effect can increase the apparent air temperature—how your body experiences that heat—by about 10° to 15°F. Those kinds of numbers can be hard to comprehend on their own, so think of it as the difference between waiting for the bus in direct sun when it's 85°F versus 100°F outside. The urban heat island effect is not isolated to daytime temperatures. As the days get hotter, the nights do, too. Dark surfaces release stored heat out into the night air, robbing people's bodies of the opportunity to cool down and relieve the physical and psychological stresses of the day's elevated temperatures. To mitigate the threat that heat poses to our com-munities, successful interventions must do three things: block, bounce, and cool.

Block

Blocking means preventing the sun from touching things and people so that they don't heat up. It can be through very short-term measures, such as erecting a shade structure over a bus stop or extending a cloth canopy over a café patio, or through longer-term measures, such as planting trees that will, once they're well established, shade homes, businesses, and sidewalks and cool the air through evapotranspiration. Evapotranspiration occurs when the sun hits the canopy of a tree, causing water to evaporate from the leaves. The energy from the sun goes into turning that water from liquid into a gas, which means that there's less energy, or heat, to warm the air. It's kind of like a tiny outside air conditioner.

In regions with hot climates, there are long-standing examples of blocking practices. For example, in Phoenix, Arizona,[4] large sheets of canvas called shade sails are suspended over public plazas or restaurant patios. In cities outside the Southwest, a drive through historically wealthy neighborhoods is likely to bring you under the cooling canopies of sturdy, mature trees.

To help reduce the utility costs of Oyler High School in the Lower Price Hill neighborhood of Cincinnati, Ohio, Groundwork Ohio River Valley installed a green roof (figure 2-1). The drought-tolerant native plants will block the summer sun, retain stormwater, and provide year-round added insulation to the building. The resources needed to shade and cool communities exist; they just might not be where you are or distributed to the areas of highest need.

Bounce

Another mitigation method is to reflect light to lessen heat absorption. We can't block everything from the sun, so our next task is

Figure 2-1: Green roof atop the Oyler High School in the Lower Price Hill neighborhood of Cincinnati, Ohio. This green roof, built by Groundwork Ohio River Valley, will reduce the temperature of the surrounding area and absorb stormwater. (Photo by Phil Heidenreich. Courtesy of Groundwork Ohio River Valley.)

to keep the ground and buildings from heating up in other ways. Darker colors absorb heat from sunlight while lighter colors reflect light away from Earth's surface, so common construction materials such as asphalt, tar, and black rubber are very good at storing and reemitting heat. To reduce the temperatures of their apartments, the affordable housing provider Westhab partnered with Groundwork Hudson Valley and community members to paint the roofs white so that light is reflected off of the building instead of being absorbed into it—an intervention that's equally as useful on smaller residential properties that currently have dark roofs.

Cool

Finally, no matter how many shade structures we erect or trees we plant, people are going to get hot, and we need ways to cool ourselves. While cooling is especially urgent during extreme events such as the heat dome that settled over the Pacific Northwest in 2021, humans are experiencing the ill effects of even moderate increases in heat. Everything from splash pads to air conditioners are needed to keep people safe from heat, but those can be tough to access on a tight budget or in an area without access to pools or spray decks. That is where higher-touch advocacy and deeper community connections come in and includes everything from donating or lending unused air-conditioning units and fans to neighbors, to inviting friends without climate control over to your house to cool off during the hotter parts of the day. Our cities need common cooling infrastructure that's accessible to everyone, but especially the most vulnerable. The discomfort and death connected to heat events is entirely preventable. From small personal decisions to larger-scale community actions, change and safety are within reach.

Fire

Fire plays a pivotal role in nature and human culture. Naturally occurring fire has been a part of the intrinsic ecology in many regions of the United States, and human-controlled fire has been an important tool for managing landscapes. For many millennia, Indigenous people across North America have practiced "cultural burning" to manage vegetation and wildlife. As Frank Kanawha Lake, a researcher with the USDA Forest Service and a Karuk descendant, explains, this practice "links back to the tribal philosophy of fire as medicine. When you prescribe it, you're getting the right dose to maintain the abundance of productivity of all ecosystem services to support the ecology in your culture."[5] In the early twentieth century, the US Forest Service moved toward suppressing all forest fires, an approach that has created landscapes prone to uncontrollable wildfires.

With unpredictable precipitation and increased bouts of extreme heat, wildfires have increased in frequency and severity, and the associated health and safety risks are problems that most people in the United States have dealt with or will deal with in the near future. If you reside in the western United States, you have lived with the dangers of wildfires. In 2020 alone, nearly 9,900 wildfires burned in California.[6] More recently, the raging 2023 Canadian wildfires covered the eastern United States in a blanket of toxic orange smoke. Fire and smoke are no longer regional issues. Instead, which risk you face from fire depends on whether or not you live in a wildland urban interface (WUI) zone—a developed area near unoccupied land such as a forest or hillside with vegetation. People and structures, like homes, in a WUI are at high risk for fire. These danger zones are not limited to western states. The states with the greatest number of homes in a WUI area are California, Texas, Florida, North Carolina, and Pennsylvania.[7] Due to extended periods of heat and drought, even communities previously unfamiliar with the phenomenon can find themselves at risk of brush fires and smoke.

So, what to do? The first step is to channel your inner Smokey Bear and lean into what you can do to prevent brush fires around your home and businesses. If you have a backyard or side yards around your home, keep them clear of dried plant matter or construction materials and consider researching landscaping options for native drought-tolerant and fire-resistant shrubs and trees. Stay on top of trimming trees that hang over your home. Pay attention to the weather report and keep an eye on your yard on days when it's both hot and windy—key conditions for brush fires. Avoid parking or idling on dry grass because parts of your car can spark or get hot enough to ignite desiccated plants. If you have an outdoor fire pit, be sure to fully extinguish coals. Postpone outdoor activities such as grilling and fireworks on dry, hot, and windy days, too.

The second step is to deal with smoke from wildfire events, even if they aren't local to you. Get familiar with websites that report on the local air quality index (AQI), a system developed by the Environmental Protection Agency (EPA) to inform the public about daily air quality. It measures the presence of five types of air pollution: ground-level ozone, carbon monoxide, sulfur dioxide, nitrogen dioxide, and particle pollution. AQI values run from 0 to 500, with readings at or below 100 generally considered satisfactory for all people to breathe. Values from 101 to 150 represent air that is unhealthy for sensitive groups such as the elderly, young children, and those with respiratory vulnerabilities such as asthma or chronic obstructive pulmonary disease. Anything above 151 is unsafe for all groups. In 2023, Canadian wildfire smoke traveled across the United States, hovering across the Northeast—at its worst one week, New York City's AQI reached a peak of 460.[8] In 2020, the San Francisco Bay Area experienced similarly apocalyptic-feeling air quality as toxic orange smoke blotted out the sun.

When wildfire smoke settles over your community, your goal is to reduce, as much as possible, your exposure to breathing in that dirty air, even if you're generally healthy. Particle pollution is a significant component of wildfire smoke and a primary health concern, especially fine particles ($PM_{2.5}$, or particulate matter 2.5 micrometers in diameter and smaller), which are small enough to embed deep into your lungs and bloodstream.[9] Researchers are still learning about the long-term health impacts of frequent exposure to wildfire smoke, but recent studies suggest that particle pollution from wildfires poses a significantly higher risk than other types of air pollution because of what is burning (cars, buildings, plastics).[10] If you have a central HVAC system or air purifiers, run them on the "fan" setting with the windows closed to filter out air; make sure to frequently service filters. If you don't have air conditioning, keeping the windows closed tight and running ceiling, standing, and box fans to circulate the internal air can also help. Finally, the use of N95 masks, a postpandemic staple in most homes, can be helpful indoors and out in keeping fine particles out of your lungs. However, it is safest to remain indoors if possible and limit physical activities outside. I want to emphasize that even though news reports and public health alerts tend to focus on the very young, elderly, and those with preexisting health conditions, breathing in any amount of wildfire smoke isn't great for anyone. The particles that get lodged in your lungs don't have a way to get back out, and it's important to keep your lungs healthy and clear as you age. If you're able to protect yourself from wildfire smoke with masks or by staying indoors, do it. That outdoor run can wait for another day.

Water

A warmer planet means a wetter atmosphere, which for some communities means more frequent and intense precipitation events. In other regions, like the semiarid southwestern United States, rising temperatures intensify the opposite risk: drought. Higher air temperatures in dryer regions, such as the western and southern United States, increase transpiration (when hotter weather removes moisture from plants and soil). Conversely, increased temperatures in wetter regions cause more evaporation; warmer air holds on to water vapor more readily than cooler air, and an atmosphere with more moisture can create more precipitation. According to the *Fourth National Climate Assessment* report, heavy precipitation events—periods of abnormally high rain or snow—have increased over the last century in every region outside of the Southwest.[11]

When rain falls at a rate that is too fast for the ground to absorb, water collects. Many cities are at high risk for flooding because paved surfaces such as sidewalks and asphalt are nonporous and because what soil cover that does exist is of poor enough quality to become impermeable or oversaturated during extended periods of intense rain. With no way to soak into the ground, water either collects and becomes stagnant or runs down into the nearest low-lying area, which might be a storm drain or inside your home.

Research suggests that our warming planet is also going to expand suitable habitats for mosquitoes and ticks that carry bacteria and viruses that can cause parasitic illnesses such as Lyme disease, alpha-gal syndrome, malaria, chikungunya, and dengue fever. Many urban communities in North America haven't had to think about these diseases for generations—if at all—but times are changing, and we need to collectively turn our attention to the lessons learned by rural communities that have battled stormwater, poor stormwater management, and heat for generations. Alabama native and environmental health researcher Catherine Coleman Flowers has, for decades, rung the alarm about the environmental injustices present in communities with poor sanitation and poor stormwater management—challenges that disproportionately impact lower-income communities and communities of color due to poor federal and state investment but that have consequences for us all. In communities without adequate sanitation, Flowers points out, there has already been a resurgence of diseases such as hookworm.[12] As heavy rainfall causes an increase of combined sewer overflow events, sewage backups, and malfunctioning septic systems, the risk of diseases previously thought to be eradicated rises. If left unaddressed, these risks will become even more pronounced and spread. In addition to disease-carrying pests and parasites, water runoff can carry motor oil, pulverized rubber from tires, and trash into our homes, into storm drains that feed to rivers, lakes, and oceans, and into our sources of drinking water. To mitigate the threat that stormwater poses to our communities, interventions need to accomplish three things: retain, absorb, and redirect. There are some individual actions you can take immediately to help reduce the impact of water on your community.

Retain

Setting up retention infrastructure, such as rain barrels, allows you to reduce the amount of stormwater that runs off your roof while holding on to water for later use around your home. Rain barrels are big receptacles attached to a gutter's downspout. The rain barrel behind my apartment building holds sixty gallons of stormwater that I use to irrigate the flowers and raspberry bushes I grow in the side yard.[13] I got it for free on my local Buy Nothing group, but these barrels can be purchased in hardware stores and online for as little as $30. You can take them with you when you move or leave them behind for the next family to enjoy.

If you don't have gutters or want to get a little artsy, consider installing rain chains (figure 2-2). They hang from your roof, and gravity draws the runoff down the chain and into decorative containers that store and slowly release the water into the air and ground. Heads up that warmer weather and stagnant water are a recipe for mosquitoes and the cornucopia of discomfort and disease that they bring with them, so be sure to treat the water in your retention structures with watershed-friendly products like mosquito dunks that naturally stave off larvae while maintaining water quality.

Figure 2-2: A rain chain in Milwaukee, Wisconsin, attached to the roof of the building. The chain funnels rainwater into a container below. (Photo by author.)

Absorb

The next intervention is absorption whereby stormwater makes its way into the soil and plants where it can be held and slowly released out into the air and underground water tables. You achieve increased absorption in three ways: (1) by improving soil health; (2) by planting or protecting greenery, such as trees or native grasses, that will soak up and retain rainwater; and (3) by removing pavement from where it doesn't really need to be. We'll talk in more detail about each of these three methods in chapter three.

Cities are doing the best they can with current infrastructure, but the increased intensity and frequency of extreme weather events like hurricanes brought about by the climate crisis is causing water to either evade or overwhelm draining and sewage systems. The way our cities are built also exacerbates flooding issues. As a result, cities rely on storm drains to carry runoff away from homes and roads to nearby bodies of water.

A few years after I moved to New England, I visited the Deer Island Wastewater Treatment Plant in Boston Harbor. For most of metropolitan Boston's history, stormwater and sewage were collected from surrounding cities and towns in underground pipes and spewed into the Charles River, the Mystic River, and Boston Harbor—a very common, and extremely gross, practice for older cities. In 1997, the Massachusetts Water Resource Authority brought Deer Island's treatment standards up to those set by the federal Clean Water Act as a means of protecting the harbor from the effects of contamination and expanded its discharge system deeper into the Atlantic.[14] The current system collects sewage and stormwater from forty cities and towns, cleans it, and then discharges it 10 miles from shore, 100 feet beneath the surface of Massachusetts Bay.

These days, most US cities have high-quality underground

stormwater management systems that capture and safely discharge stormwater. But that water first must get into the sewer system, and the sewer has to be big enough to handle that water without overflowing. In my climate organizing work, the most common complaint from residents has had to do with flooding.[15] In San Diego, California, residents along the Chollas Creek watershed have long suffered the effects of flash floods and overflowing storm basins. In New Jersey, Union County's combined sewer system can result in neighborhood streets covered in untreated sewage when the stormwater system overflows into the residential and commercial sewage system, mixing together and discharging into local waterways.[16] In suburban Rhode Island, sewage sometimes backs up through ground-floor toilets, ruining carpets, furniture, and clothing and kicking off blooms of harmful mold in drywall.

While extreme weather events can overwhelm storm drainage systems, even less severe rain can cause disruptive flooding if water cannot reach the storm drains because debris is blocking its path. A small action anyone can take is to clear obstacles from your neighborhood storm drains.

I took a photo of a storm drain while walking my daughter to daycare one morning (figure 2-3); instead of a clear route from the street to the sewer, years of compacted dirt and flourishing weeds had plugged the drain and kept water from draining into the sewers. One tiny way to help? Clear the blockage. Some cities have adopt-a-drain programs that encourage community engagement in maintaining storm drains. When the Bay Area experienced record-breaking rainfall during the winter of 2022, San Francisco residents signed up for the San Francisco Public Utilities Commission's (SFPUC) drain adoption program. In return, volunteers got equipment to clear debris and, most excitingly, the right to name their storm drain—a particularly rich incentive for pun

Figure 2-3: Dirt, trash, and plants can block the flow of water from the street into the sewer system. Clearing out debris from storm drains is a simple action to reduce local flooding. (Photo by author.)

enthusiasts. Exploring SFPUC's adopt-a-drain map will reveal city storm basins with monikers such as "It's Draining Men," "Thirsty Boi," and "You're So Drain."[17]

In our case, I found a stick, and my daughter and I squatted on the sidewalk to scrape and pull the plants and clods of dirt out of the grate, clearing the path for the rain to drain from our neighborhood to Deer Island. Even the smallest of us can contribute to creating climate safe neighborhoods.

Unequal Distribution of Risk

As we learned in chapter one, the way our neighborhoods look is not accidental. The discriminatory legacy of redlining, urban renewal, and highway placement in US cities affects how communities experience climate risks, and it is no surprise that racial and ethnic minorities are disproportionately affected. An EPA report from 2021 studied the climate vulnerability of certain segments of the population—based on income, age, race, and ethnicity—and found that Black people faced higher impacts from the climate crisis in all six categories measured, including air quality, extreme temperatures, weather-related disruptions to income, and flooding.[18] People who identified as Hispanic and Latino were 43 percent more likely to live in areas where weather-related events such as wildfire smoke or excessive rain negatively impacted access or ability to work and earn income.[19]

Once we begin noting the connection between our built environment and climate risks, we can focus our efforts and find people with whom we can drive solutions. When you're equipped with a climate-focused lens through which to view and understand your neighborhood, certain priorities are likely to rise to the top—simple ones like the need to clear a path for water to get to the storm drain or more complex ones like the need for more greenspace. This awareness will help you assess which issues you'd like to prioritize and how you might like to get involved: as an individual making changes to your block or as part of a group advocating for change at the city or state level.

At whatever level you get involved, change will be more of an uphill battle in some places than in others. Neighborhoods that are or were historically lower income or majority minority tend to be hotter and wetter than other areas because fewer cooling, drying greenspaces are sited there by municipal officials. Fewer trees line the sidewalks and medians because of intentional decisions at the federal, state, and municipal levels to invest in some neighborhoods rather than others. In these communities, you're not only setting out to overcome the climate risk embedded in the built and natural environments; you're also setting a course toward changing how decisions are made, resources distributed, and equality realized. Luckily, the path to climate safer neighborhoods has some simple, easy-to-achieve interventions that we'll explore in the next chapter.

CHAPTER 3

Now What? Small Solutions

Now that you're thoroughly bummed about why our communities look the way they do and how deadly and destructive climate risks like heat and flooding can be, let's get to the good part: what you can do about it.

One step you can take is to observe your community and collect information. I don't mean heading out there with clipboards and calibrated sensors (we'll get to that in chapter seven). I mean simply noticing the built and natural environment as you go about your day-to-day life. Start by asking yourself some questions related to heat, drought, flood, and fire. How does your neighborhood change across the seasons? During heavy rain events, does water collect anywhere, such as in your yard or inside your home? Do intersections flood? When it's hot, how do you feel while walking in your neighborhood or waiting at the bus stop? Where are the trees planted? Are there "enough" of them to cool the area? How much pavement and soil are in your community? How healthy is the soil that is there? Is it soft and able to absorb water, or is it hard and prone to runoff?

All cities have pavement and trees, and the amount of each affects how your community experiences climate risks. Nonporous paved surfaces, whether asphalt or concrete, are one of the biggest obstacles to battling the urban heat island effect and stormwater flooding. Meanwhile, mature trees cool our environments and increase the soil's ability to absorb water. Concentrating your efforts on pavement and trees has the added benefit of addressing several problems at the same time: blocking and bouncing the sun's energy to reduce heat and redirecting, absorbing, and retaining water to reduce flood risk. This chapter will focus on direct actions you can take as an individual to limit pavement and increase tree cover in your community.

Pull It Up

Why do cities use so much pavement, particularly asphalt, in the first place? The short answer is transportation, especially cars. Asphalt was already used for roads in the United States by the late nineteenth century, but the demand significantly increased alongside the rise of the automobile. Today, cars continue to dictate the placement of asphalt, whether for highways, roads, or parking lots. Asphalt has several benefits as a construction material that makes it popular. It's cheap, it's smooth, it sets quickly, it can easily be replaced when it reaches the end of its usable life, and the warmth it collects and stores from the sun can help keep roads clear of frost and light snow. No wonder the United States has around 2.5 million miles of its roadways paved in the stuff![1] But we don't need as much as we have, where we have it. At first glance, it's tough to see how you might impact something like the ground. What's below your feet was likely put down long before you came on the scene, so it's natural to think it'll be there long after you're gone. But small changes to this part of the built environment are within your reach and are incredibly impactful.

First, take notice of where pavement appears in your neighborhood beyond the road. Start with your immediate surroundings—your home—and work your way outward. If you have a car, where is it parked? In a driveway or parking lot? Do you have greenspace surrounding where you live, like a yard or communal area? Can you see or touch soil, or is it mostly covered in pavement? Once you take stock of where pavement appears (or doesn't), identify which of these spaces are within your direct control. For many of you, that will be your driveway.

Driveways

If you have a paved driveway and it must stay, at some point you'll need to repave it. Before you pour down more blacktop, explore other creative options that get you a solid surface for your car or basketball game without increasing flood risk around your home. What you choose depends on how much maintenance you can tolerate and where you live. Permeable pavers are a popular alternative to asphalt and poured concrete driveways, and they come in a variety of materials, such as brick and concrete blocks (figure 3-1). They also work well in different regions. If you've seen old cobblestone roads, you've seen one type of permeable paving. The pavers, whether brick, stone, or concrete, are separated by "joints" of crushed aggregate, such as gravel and sand. When it rains, the water falls between these grooves and is absorbed into the ground instead of running off or collecting on the surface. Real talk: permeable driveways and walkways that use a combination of pavers and small stones can be expensive to install and difficult to maintain. Weeds can grow between the cracks, and ground settling can

Figure 3-1: The spaces between the pavers and the grate at the end of this permeable driveway provide a path for stormwater to enter the ground. (Photo by author.)

make the surface uneven. Some types of permeable pavers need to have the joints vacuumed once a year to remove debris and ensure water can percolate through the ground. If you're not into vacuuming your outdoor surfaces, grass pavers are a reasonable alternative for a relatively low maintenance driveway or walkway, though they're best suited for regions that get regular rain and snow. These sheets of interconnected hexagons are laid down on top of soil to create a driveway or patio. Grass or durable plants are placed in each cylinder, providing enough structure to support your vehicle and withstand stressors like snow removal while creating a cooling, water-absorbing surface.

If permeable isn't possible, consider reducing the square footage of impermeable pavement. You could also consider installing two thin paving strips for car tires to drive on and leaving the rest of the space planted with hearty grasses. Another option is paving with light-colored material. That won't address stormwater runoff or flooding, but it will help reflect the sun's energy and reduce the urban heat island effect around your home.

Depaving Parties

In communities across the United States, residents who are interested in protecting their neighborhood from heat or flood are holding "depaving parties" (figure 3-2). Even though I've been doing climate adaptation work for years, I was only recently invited to my first neighborhood depaving party. Crystal Bordewieck, a resident living just a few blocks from my apartment, reached out to our local climate coalition to ask for help pulling up the black-top outside of her back door. The Green and Open Coalition, a team of community members who joined together to reduce pavement in our city, sent out a digital blast to the neighborhood via our city's climate coalition listserv asking volunteers to show up

Figure 3-2: Depaving party, 2022. When pulling up asphalt, expect to find gravel that was used to level the area. Depaving can reduce the urban heat island effect and local flooding by allowing plants and soil to reflect solar radiation and absorb stormwater. (Photo by author.)

with closed-toed shoes and a water bottle. An avid gardener, my neighbor spends much of the year growing fruits, vegetables, and herbs in containers to donate to our local mutual aid society. The previous owners had paved over the entire backyard, so she didn't have space for a larger gardening setup. But with more soil accessible, she would have room to plant marigolds and nasturtiums, both natural pest deterrents to the aphids and squash beetles that tend to plague gardeners. She could also expand the quantity and types of crops she grew while reducing her home's contribution to the urban heat island effect and local flooding.

When I arrived to help depave, I was greeted by a cross between a block party and a construction site. The first thing I saw as I approached the house was a dumpster parked on the street outside. A barrel full of thick gloves, goggles, and hard-hats sat next to a stack of long crowbars and wooden blocks used for leverage. On the porch, tables were covered with pizzas, bowls of popcorn, pitchers of iced tea, and nearby, a speaker playing pop covers. After a quick safety and instruction briefing, we were off! Ten strangers (and a city councilor from the neighboring ward who just wanted to lend a hand) donned safety equipment, and within two hours we had completely stripped three layers of asphalt down to the soil. For the cost of a dumpster permit and a few pizzas, the homeowner had access to plantable, water-absorbing soil for the first time.

Depaving parties can strengthen both your climate resilience and your connection to your neighbors. Reflecting on the experience, Crystal credits the event with making her feel closer to members of the community. "You know how after the first time you meet someone it's easier to reach out to them after? Connecting was a lot easier after the depaving party," she says. Forming these relationships also opened the door for her to get involved in other projects around the neighborhood. These parties are simple volunteer opportunities that turn climate mitigation into memorable events and can bring a community together around an achievable goal. Besides the satisfying feeling of peeling off a long strip of asphalt, one of my favorite things about depaving parties is that almost anyone can participate. While much of the action is around prying up blacktop, there are plenty of roles for people of most ages and abilities: drumming up volunteers via email, playing music to keep depavers' energy up, entertaining young children so that parents can participate, refilling water bottles, passing out safety equipment, ordering pizzas, or helping to plant flowers in the newly exposed soil. Note that asphalt leaves contaminants behind in the dirt, so you should never directly plant food for human consumption prior to remediating the soil. Flowers, grass, trees, and decorative plants, however, are just fine!

You can learn more at Depave.org, a nonprofit organization providing resources and education about concrete and asphalt removal. Depave is based in Portland, Oregon, but people have formed affiliate groups in places such as Detroit, Cleveland, and Nashville. The groups partner with local schools, religious institutions, community groups, and other nonprofits to remove paved surfaces. They rely on volunteers, so you do not need to own property to participate in depaving efforts. If you cannot find a local group working on this issue and you'd like to start your own, reach out to the folks at Depave. They have plenty of experience explaining the process and helping communities get started by training others on safe ways to peel asphalt, how to apply for grant funding for materials such as crowbars and helmets, and how to conduct effective outreach.

Soil Quality

Even if you remove pavement, sometimes the ground below isn't much better. My apartment building was originally constructed to house workers for the local brick and lead smelting factories. The soil in the surrounding yard is clay-heavy and, after decades of neglect, is compacted and nearly impervious to water. If a person could muster the strength to jam a shovel through an inch or two of the hard surface, they would uncover a stiff wedge of earth and clay flecked with small stones. Soil like this is not quite as harmful as asphalt, but it's pretty close. When it rains, the dirt is too compressed to absorb water, which rolls straight onto our neighbor's driveway. In the summer, we miss out on the cooling benefits of evapotranspiration because the soil is too hard and nutrient sparse to accommodate plant growth.

Healthy soil has insects and fungi decomposing plant and animal matter into nutrients and traps greenhouse gases such as carbon dioxide. Plants have roots that aerate the soil, absorb and retain water, and prevent soil erosion. Improving the soil quality by aerating it, adding nutrients, and seeding nitrogen-fixing plants improves the soil's ability to protect your community from heat and flooding. Healthy soil needs a few things: air, insects, microbes, water, and organic matter—all things that you can help reintroduce over time. A relatively low-effort way to improve soil health either by yourself or with friends and neighbors is to let plants do the heavy lifting on aerating and adding nutrients to the ground.

Cover Crops

If you went to elementary school in the United States, you probably heard about the agricultural chemist George Washington Carver at some point during the month of February. While he's frequently known as the "peanut guy," he made brilliant contributions to agriculture and to our scientific understanding of conserving and returning nutrients to the soil. Many indigenous cultures that practice agriculture have contributed a tremendous amount to knowledge of soil health; Carver's research furthered American agriculturalists' understanding of how cover crops can restore health to overworked, neglected, and poor-quality soil.

Cover crops are plants such as clover, buckwheat, hairy vetch, and peas that slow down the erosion of topsoil, add vital nutrients via their roots, reduce soil compaction and increase water absorption, and add organic matter to the topsoil through the decomposition of leaves and stems once the plant dies. These plants aren't eaten, but instead they're grown and then turned over into the soil at the end of the season, providing additional nutrients to the ground.

If you have access to a patch of soil, such as a yard or space between the sidewalk and the road, that could use a nutrient or aeration boost, spread cover crop seeds at the beginning or very end of the summer and let nature do the work. Cover crops are relatively easy to put down—you just need a shovel to flip or a pitchfork to loosen the soil and then scatter the seeds across the ground. Wait for the crops to grow, and when they reach maturity, turn the plants over into the soil to decompose. When a plant has reached maturity depends on the type of cover crop, but in most regions of the United States, it is a safe bet that if you plant in May or June, the plants will be mature enough to fold into the soil by early September.

To learn about native cover crops for your region, you can find information online or at a public library. Most state university agricultural programs publish lists of native cover crops on their website and have professors or extension specialists at community support centers who will be happy to answer your questions via phone or email. You can purchase seeds online, at a local nursery, or sometimes even directly from university agricultural programs. Alternatively, if you can't find native seeds, you can plant commercially available backyard cover crops such as vetch, clover, winter peas, annual ryegrass, oats, and winter wheat—just know that some common cover crops such as cow vetch are considered invasive in some regions, so you'll want to flip them before they seed and avoid using them if you live near a conservation area.

You can also spread cover crops over underutilized land by hurling seed bombs wherever soil improvement is needed. This method is more hands-off than planting cover crops on soil you can tend directly, but it's quick, it's relatively easy, and it actually makes for a pretty fun activity with friends or family members.

SEED BOMB RECIPE

1 cup of cover crop or wildflower seeds

3 cups of clay powder or soil (If you have clay-heavy soil like I do, you can just pop outside, dig up some clay, and use that instead; make sure to wear a mask when disturbing soil you're not familiar with.)

6 cups of compost (If you can't make your own, store bought is fine.)

Water

Mix the dry ingredients together and then slowly add water until you get a shaggy biscuit dough consistency. Roll the mixture into balls and let them dry on paper in a sunny window. When they are dry, wrap some up and take them with you on a walk with friends or give them away to others. Throw a few anywhere you see the soil needing a little love throughout the spring, summer, and early fall, depending on the seed type.

Composting

A steady source of compost is an easy way to rejuvenate soil, making it more capable of cooling the surrounding air and absorbing stormwater. Even if you do not need compost for your own soil, composting that limp carrot languishing in your crisper is a way to return the vegetable's carbon to the soil instead of adding it to the food waste in landfills. If you garden or are looking to revitalize the soil around your building, each onion peel and apple core you throw into the garbage is free fertilizer that you're sending away each week. An estimated 30 to 40 percent of the country's food supply goes to waste, and most of it ends up in landfills or incinerators. Not only are these trash facilities as a whole major sources of greenhouse gas emissions, but they also pollute the neighborhoods they are in, which are most often communities of color.[2]

You can effectively compost no matter how much time or space you have available. If you live in one of a handful of cities that offers municipal composting, your city does most of the heavy lifting for you; you just need to separate out your compostable waste from your trash and recycling. At this point, most cities do not offer citywide curbside compost pickup. If you do want to compost but do not want to maintain a compost pile or bin yourself, other options are available. Increasingly, for-profit and not-for-profit enterprises are offering porch-pickup services. For a monthly fee, they give you a big bucket to collect your food scraps. Then, about once per week, the organization hauls it away, replacing it with a sparkling clean bucket. For a free option, check to see if your local farmers' market, grocery store, or community garden accepts food scrap drop-offs.

Maintaining a compost bin can seem daunting at first. Compost bins have a reputation for being stinky, temperamental, and prone to attracting undesirable critters such as rats and racoons. Those aren't lies, but with a little advanced planning, these quickly become nonissues. Whether you live in an apartment with no outdoor space or a house with a yard, you can choose from a variety of composting methods. A friend of mine swears he's got the most beautiful flower bed in the entire city of Milwaukee, Wisconsin, thanks to vermicomposting. In his basement he's got some bins with shredded paper, food scraps, and a colony of red earthworms that produce light, fluffy compost. This style is definitely for the composting enthusiast as the benefits you gain from its small footprint are balanced out by the care and attention you need to give to keep the bin and earthworms healthy. Barrel and bin composting are lower maintenance than vermicomposting but do require more space. Searching online or at your public library for tips on composting is a good way to learn more about the style that works best for your situation.

Trees: The Best Bang for Your Buck

Paying attention to what is beneath your feet will help you take care of the most important tool for reducing climate risks in your neighborhood: trees. Trees are a powerful way to put a barrier between your community and the consequences of the climate crisis. They are a protective piece of infrastructure that needs to get just as much attention as a road, rail line, or sidewalk.

The first thing to know is that life is hard out there for an urban tree! In a forest, tree roots can stretch and connect to one another through a complex fungal network. Through this system, scientists believe trees can share nutrients and even sound the alarm about threats like drought or insect invasions.[3] In contrast, the average street tree is isolated in a sidewalk box that is around 3 feet by 6 feet. City trees are exposed to climate change risks, like flooding, drought, and extreme heat, as well as hazards such as damage from construction and development expansion. A study by the US Forest Service estimates that urban communities lose about thirty-six million trees per year, much of that to property redevelopment.[4] Some cities, like Cleveland, have seen tree canopy loss of more than 50 percent since the 1950s and are projected to lose more, even with robust tree-planting efforts from the public and nonprofit sectors.[5] Urban trees need all the help they can get. Even if you are not an arborist, there are ways you can preserve and increase tree canopy in your community.

Tree Planting

The city of Central Falls, located just outside of Providence, Rhode Island, is a working-class, formerly redlined community with large immigrant populations from Cape Verde, Liberia, and the Dominican Republic, among others. Until recently, the city distributed new trees on a first-come, first-serve basis using an English-only online application. Those in the know, mostly wealthier English speakers with internet access, were able to hop on the website each spring and claim the trees at the start of the planting season, leaving the hotter, lower-income neighborhoods barren. Groundwork Rhode Island, residents, and public health providers pulled together to ask the tree warden to rethink the distribution policy and distribute trees based on community need. Thanks to resident advocacy and the openness of the city, the city now seeks out opportunities to proactively plant trees with partners in areas with the greatest need and uses the American Forest's Tree Equity Score to guide their planting.

How does your municipality choose to distribute its trees? You can likely find your city's tree planning approach online and might want to ask a few questions about it. When was the tree plan last updated? How does your city distribute trees? Does it specifically prioritize planting in vulnerable neighborhoods? Chapter six will cover in more detail how to work with your city councilor and other stakeholders to make systems-level changes in your community. You'll be able to apply those lessons to influence how and where trees are planted in your community.

But you don't have to wait for your city to distribute trees. There are ways to get involved, either as an individual or along with neighbors, to plant more trees in your community. Even if you have limited opportunity, or none at all, for tree planting around your home, you likely have relationships with friends and family who might, with a little nudging, have room for a tree. Another sphere of influence to keep in mind includes community groups and associations you belong to, such as local schools or religious institutions. Whether you plan to plant trees on your own property, help friends or neighbors plant, or influence larger-scale planting in your neighborhood, it's important to understand what your community needs and what your city requires. There are a number of details to consider, including species, surroundings, and depth.

Most cities with urban forestry goals will only achieve them by planting both in the public right-of-way and on private property. As mentioned above, there are some residents who, for very good reasons, are not interested in trees. That's where relationship building comes in. Tennis Lilly, an arborist in the Merrimack Valley of Massachusetts, spends a lot of his time getting to know residents, listening to their concerns, and discussing the benefits and drawbacks to tree planting. Tennis tells me it can take two to three planting seasons' worth of conversation with residents to fully understand their perspective and assess if a tree is right for their yard or if it's totally a no-go. If you're speaking to your neighbors about trees, make sure you're doing more listening than talking. You can share your own personal experience with the benefits of trees, but be respectful.

Right Tree, Right Place

A tree might be an ideal way to cool a community, but in the wrong location it can block the sun for a garden where a family grows hard-to-come-by vegetables and herbs that connect them to their culture or provide additional food security. No one is looking for extra chores, and the drop of leaves in the autumn is a gift that keeps on giving for six or more weeks a year. Fruit trees can be messy, and if you want to hear people get creative with describing smells, chat with those who live near female ginkgo trees.[6] I say all this not to discourage you, but to note that planting new trees requires some research and planning.

If you have the space to plant a tree in a location you control, choose a variety that has a good chance of survival in your part of the country and requires a level of attention you're willing and able to give it. If your municipality, or one nearby, has a list of native trees, that's a good place to start. You can reach out to professionals in your urban forestry division for their opinion (and sometimes they'll even give you a free tree of that variety!) or hop online and search for information about local native trees from reputable sources, such as a local university's extension program or your city's urban forestry site. There are lots of YouTube videos that will run you through everything from choosing your tree to pruning it during the first three years. Better yet, if you live near a tree nursery, the skilled professionals there can give you some great advice.

Find a native tree that's suitable not only for the current environmental conditions where you live but that has a better chance of thriving under future conditions. The future conditions projection is tough for even expert arborists to gauge, but organizations such as the US Department of Agriculture and the Climate Change Response Framework maintain tree species projections online, essentially a digital list of trees that are likely to do well in changing climate conditions for each region. Fall and spring are generally the best times to plant a tree in most parts of the country. In summer, the stress of hot days, intense sun, and infrequent rain can kill the tree, as can the sharp cold and low light in winter.

In addition to making sure your tree gets the sun it needs and offers you the benefits you desire (for example, shade, privacy, fruit), make sure you consider the restrictions around where you want to plant it. Look for and avoid low-hanging power lines that branches will get tangled up in as they grow. In most municipalities, the power company has the authority to cut down or dramatically trim any trees that threaten its infrastructure (figure 3-3). While older trees would have been exempted from such cuts around the power lines because they provide more benefits than new trees, new plantings are kept away from power lines entirely. If you must plant near power lines, choose slow-growing, columnar, or miniature varieties.

Check out figure 3-4, a photo of a newly planted tree. In about fifteen years, this scraggly sapling is going to be an incredibly valuable asset to the community, but for now the shade it casts is about the size and shape of a pizza box. As it grows, the tree's impact will be limited by its surroundings. Directly above it are power lines, so all the new sidewalk trees on this block are slow-growing miniature varieties that will plateau at about 20 feet in height. The two upper floors of the adjacent triple-decker buildings will likely never benefit from the tree's shade, but pedestrians will.

What is beneath the street also influences where trees should be planted. In homes that use natural gas for cooking and heating, an underground pipe usually runs from the road, under the sidewalk, to the building. The heat radiating from gas and sewage pipes can attract the tree's roots, setting you up for a costly repair. Steer clear of planting within 5 to 10 feet of those lines—if your community has sidewalks, there's often a small metal box submerged in the cement marked with a "G" or the name of your local utility company that marks the location of the gas line. If you're still unsure, call your local Dig Safe line by dialing 811. That said, finding a gas-free spot can be a challenge because of the prevalence of natural gas pipes in the United States. Even if you do avoid planting

Figure 3-3: A tree trimmed away from power lines by the local energy company. (Photo by author.)

Figure 3-4: A Princess Diana serviceberry sapling planted in a sidewalk box. This tree is a slow-growing varietal, thus avoiding damage to power lines above and infrastructure below ground. (Photo by author.)

too close to a line, aging pipe infrastructure means you should still be vigilant about potential leaks.

The United States has a complex network of underground pipes, around half of which were installed in the 1950s and 1960s, that distribute natural gas to homes and businesses. These pipes are prone to cracks and leaks at the joint, and they can be expensive to repair, so utility companies are hesitant to fix them unless they are an explosion risk. It's estimated that about 2.3 percent of natural gas that's produced leaks out into the atmosphere through cracks in gas transmission lines.[7] The older your city, the more likely it is to have leaky gas infrastructure. For example, the Boston metro area loses up to 4.7 percent of the methane pumped through its natural gas infrastructure annually to leaks—the emissions equivalent of 250,000 cars running nonstop for a year.[8] Not only do leaks release tremendous amounts of methane, a potent greenhouse gas, into a system that's already warming at an alarming rate, but even small amounts of natural gas can smother roots, quickly killing the tree. Use your nose to identify leaks in natural gas infrastructure (natural gas is odorless, but an additive, which smells like rotten egg, is used to alert people to leaks). Look up the natural gas emergency report line for your local utility provider and pop that number into your phone so that it's easy to call in a leak for repair while you're on the go. Make sure to note the street address closest to where you smell the leak so that the operator knows where to send the gas line technician. And be persistent—sometimes it takes multiple calls to get a technician out and the leak identified.

Microforests, Macroimpact

If you want to scale up, look for opportunities to bring denser tree canopies to your community. In most cities, land is at a premium, and setting aside large swaths for a forest is practically impossible. Enter the microforest!

Gaining popularity from Sarasota, Florida, to Seattle, Washington, microforests are a great way to restore or maintain underutilized land and in just five years can provide the same flood control, cooling, and air quality benefits of a fifty-year-old forest of the same size.[9] The microforest, or Miyawaki forest, named after the Japanese botanist who popularized the technique, is made of hundreds of densely planted native trees, shrubs, and ground cover to create a multitiered urban forest in a space as small as three parking spots (about 300 square feet).

Microforests provide major benefits from a tree conservation perspective. Trees planted in microforests benefit from the nutrient network shared by other trees, plants, and fungi and from the cooling effect caused by other plants' evapotranspiration. Additionally, they create beautiful community spaces that support "a greater diversity of birds and wildlife and become[] a special destination for residents and visitors to enjoy," explains Sarasota Audubon president Jeanne Dubi, referring to the small forest a coalition of volunteers planted in Bradenton, Florida.[10]

Groups that have ownership over parcels of underutilized land, such as schools, religious institutions, and community centers, might consider bringing the benefits of wild locations into the city.[11] Elizabeth, New Jersey, is a dense, busy, and energetic city just a thirty-minute train ride from New York's Penn Station. Home to the largest seaport on the East Coast, the city struggles with poor air quality and with flooding from the ocean, from groundwater, and from the Elizabeth River. Groundwork Elizabeth has planted five microforests on small, unused, and contaminated plots of land with terrible soil quality. Just a few months after planting, the nonprofit's staff was giving a tour of the newest site when the owner of the greengrocer next door came out of his shop to share the news that his store's basement, which had been prone to flooding that destroyed goods, hadn't seen any water since the installation of the microforest—a big deal for his bottom line. Partner with your city, school, workplace, or religious institution and look for opportunities to reuse underused land for community benefit through tree planting.

Tree Preservation: Why It Matters

When I moved to New England, my first job was working for my state's public housing agency. Our division oversaw around 240 locally run "authorities" that provided public housing, mostly to low-income seniors. One local housing authority had several tall, sturdy trees surrounding each building on the campus. Those beautiful maples, oaks, and honey locusts dropped a tremendous amount of leaves each year—we're talking literal truckloads—and were a total pain for the small number of maintenance staff to stay on top of when they already had hundreds of units to manage with a shoestring staff. To reduce the amount of time and money spent on leaf-focused grounds keeping, the maintenance team cut down many of the older trees and mulched them into wood chips for the paths and flower beds.

A few weeks after the last tree was felled and the stumps ground to dust, our office received a call from the local housing authority staff. The prior night, an unusually heavy spring rain had fallen, and the buildings' basements had flooded. Many of the furnaces, central electrical panels, and water heaters—all stored in the basements—were damaged. With a single storm, the housing authority was looking at thousands of dollars in electrical expenses, and residents were staring down days of interrupted services.

Mature trees can absorb and hold between 100 and 150 gallons of water each during a rainstorm. Without trees surrounding the buildings, most of the water that ran off rooftops and out of downspouts could not be absorbed by the soil. Instead, the ground became waterlogged, and the excess water flowed over the nearby asphalt parking lot and the adjacent concrete walkway. Without anywhere else to go, water continued toward the lowest point it could find—in this case, the basement.

The issue here wasn't just that trees were removed, but that *mature* trees were removed. It might seem like the solution here is to replant the trees (which absolutely should happen!), but it takes time for trees to become useful. Saplings are like baby birds—scrawny and sparse—coasting on their potential to eventually become beautiful. With a fully grown tree, the broad canopy bounces rain around, slowing its descent, and when that water eventually reaches the ground, deep, sturdy roots absorb gallons of rainwater. The time it takes for a tree to get large enough to effectively mitigate flooding or offer shade varies from region to region. Temperature, soil composition, and hours of sunlight all impact tree growth rate. Generally, if you're east of the Mississippi River, the farther south you are, the faster trees will grow. In some places, such as northern Florida, you can get a closed canopy overhead in as little as ten years with the right species. In colder, darker climates, it's going to take three to four times as long to get the full climate adaptation benefits of a tree. For these reasons, it's important to help preserve the trees you already have in your community.

Street Tree Responsibility

Trees planted in the public right-of-way (for example, next to or within sidewalks) are usually either the responsibility of the person who owns the land next to it or the municipality. I have a neighbor who isn't thrilled about the trees on our block. While some might see the potential for shade and air filtration, she sees leaves to rake and roots to trip over. Our urban forestry department is responsible for planting and maintaining sidewalk trees within their first three years, but it's not entirely clear who is supposed to care for trees after they are established. In general, urban forestry departments, if they exist at all, are small divisions within your municipality that don't have the staff to look out for the health and wellness of every tree all the time. Some cities and counties, such as Denver, Colorado, put tree maintenance costs and responsibilities on the shoulders of residents, who sometimes didn't ask for that tree in the first place. Trees can be challenging to maintain due to their torrent of dropped leaves in the fall or the way their roots can buckle the sidewalks and create a tripping hazard and costly sidewalk repairs. Keeping trees healthy can seem daunting, especially if you are not an expert or do not have extra resources, like time and money, to spend on street trees. In Denver, for example, if residents want the street tree to survive, they're responsible for watering it, hiring an arborist to investigate illness or rot, trimming branches that are dead or in the way of the sidewalk or road, and repairing the sidewalk if a mature tree's roots crack or shift the concrete; if they don't, they face a fine. Otherwise, residents are free to ignore the trees, and if one dies—which is very likely without constant watering and care in the first three years—residents can either remove the dead tree at their own expense or leave it as a memorial to arboreal neglect. Given all that, it's not surprising that some people, like my neighbor, would not be excited about trees. But why do many cities put this responsibility on property owners?

During the Great Recession of 2008 and beyond, municipal budgets imploded, and one of the first line items to go, if it existed in the first place, was urban forestry. Tree planting ground to a halt, some cities transitioned maintenance responsibility of street trees to property owners, and trees that were ill or posed any threat were preventatively cut down instead of treated. Municipalities across the United States suffered significant canopy loss from disease, invasive species, and lack of care.

Whether you are a property owner or not, it is a good idea to know who is responsible for tree maintenance in your city so that you know how to handle tree problems (or who to give a verbal or written high-five for their great work). Here are some steps for information gathering:

1. Your city government's website is a good place to start, or you can search online for "right-of-way trees" and your city. You can also find out who is responsible for public trees by calling your municipality's main line.
2. If your city is responsible for trees, identify how to reach the appropriate person or department in charge. It might be an urban forestry department, city arborist, tree warden, or public works department.
3. If the trees are the property owner's responsibility and if that person is you, learn which trees are under your care by confirming your property lines. Many counties allow you to access property line maps online, or you can visit your county's recorder or assessor's office.
4. Find out what aspects of tree maintenance fall to property owners in your area—every municipality is different. Most cities include this information along with resources on their websites.

The Care and Feeding of Local Trees

Even if you are not a homeowner or your city takes responsibility for street trees, you can help preserve trees in your community. At

the beginning of this chapter, I said that observing your environment is the first step. Observe the trees that you frequently pass so
you can keep an eye on their health. Do this with trees in the public right-of-way (such as sidewalks and parks) and those around
your home, work, or school. Take note of how the trees change in
the late spring, summer, and early fall. Keep in mind that decidu-
ous trees will change leaf color and shed leaves seasonally, whereas
evergreens, as their name implies, keep their green foliage throughout the year. Here is what to take notice of:

- *Leaves.* Leaf color and density are appropriate for season and
  type of tree. Healthy trees have a dense crown of leaves (or
  needles). Trees in distress might have discolored, patchy, wilt-
  ing, bumpy, or mildew-covered leaves and unseasonably bare
  branches or gaps in the canopy. If most leaves have holes, the
  tree could have a pest infestation.
- *Branches.* Healthy trees are full of foliage without bare patches.
  A tree may be in trouble if it has an excessive number of dead
  or broken branches or has thin branches (also called "suck-
  ers") growing from the base of the tree trunk.
- *Trunks.* The tree bark shouldn't be loose or crumbly, except
  for certain species like eucalyptus or birch. Keep an eye out
  for gouges or holes because they could lead to pest infestation
  or disease.[12]

Just like people, trees look a little different as they age. The
smooth, light gray, resin-pocked bark of a Douglas fir becomes
brown, thick, and deeply furrowed over time, so don't be alarmed
if you notice variations in trees from year to year. If you have access to a smartphone, there are dozens of tree identification apps
that can help you learn what trees are along your route, how they
change over time, and what the specific signs are of health or

disease. If you're looking to submerge even deeper into the world of a dendrophile, the technical term for a tree lover, the agriculture and forestry divisions of local state universities often publish field guides, webinars, and books on trees to help you sharpen your identification and monitoring skills.

If there's a young tree along your route, check to see that it's planted and cared for correctly. Don't know the age of the tree? It's safe to assume it's on the younger side if the trunk's diameter is smaller than an eighteen-ounce oatmeal canister. That's not the case for all species; some maintain small trunks into maturity, but you're likely not an arborist, so just do the best you can. If the roots of a young tree are sticking out, call or email the company or agency in charge of the tree and let them know your observations; even if the tree is the responsibility of the homeowners, most municipalities have warranties with their tree planters to replace improperly planted trees within the first few years. If a tree in the public right-of-way is obviously dead—no leaves in the summer, crumbly bark—you can call the municipality and request that the dead tree be removed and replaced. Your municipality's tree people are busy. It might take several emails and calls to get on their radar—be patient, polite, and persistent. It took me several emails and calls to get the city to consider planting trees on my block, and I live in a relatively responsive city with a great urban forester.

Keep the soil around your trees clear of waste. All trees need decomposing organic material, such as their own leaves, fungus, or weeds, to bring in extra nutrients and keep the surrounding soil healthy and light. To help, clear the path for that good stuff to degrade into the soil by cleaning out trash, rocks, bricks, or debris that can get in the way. Similarly, if you have a dog, encourage your pup to avoid peeing or pooping in the tree boxes, especially in those of younger trees. Dogs' urine can kill off important soil microbes, robbing the tree's roots of important nutrients, and since canines are carnivores, their feces is slower to decompose than that of herbivores or of plant debris and offers little benefit to the tree.

Water trees of any age during droughts or during particularly hot weather. Increasing temperatures means that trees are under a tremendous amount of physical stress, and helping them out during heat waves and droughts can help take some of the pressure off. Ideally, during a drought the average tree would be watered each week to the tune of 10 gallons of water per inch of the tree trunk's diameter. But every little bit helps. If water is too expensive, you don't have a hose on the ground floor, or you can't carry a bucket back and forth (or convince friends or family members to carry it for you), even filling an old gallon milk jug and emptying that into the tree-watering bag or a tree box a few times a week will help the tree survive droughts. A tree-watering bag, sometimes called a gator bag, is a green or black plastic sack or ring that is wrapped around the tree's base. Those bags usually hold around 20 gallons of water and are used to provide a slow, deep, and focused watering to the tree as it gets established. Usually folks get rid of the bags by the third or fourth year after the tree's planting so that the tree is encouraged to stretch its roots out to find water on its own. It's OK to refill those bags during hot weather if they're empty!

You can also **add a little bit of mulch** around the base of a tree. Mulch will help the soil around the tree retain water and keep it from getting compacted so that water and gases can flow freely. Mulch only needs to be 2 inches deep and should not touch the trunk. Occasionally, people like to pile soil, compost, or mulch directly against the tree's trunk; it looks nice, but it is bad news and can lead to trunk and root rot. Make sure the area around the base of the tree is flat and unobstructed. If you see mulch piled up against a tree's trunk, clear it away with either your shoe or a stick before reforming it into a bowl shape around the trunk.

A Team Effort

You don't have to do these things alone. Taking care of trees in your neighborhood can be a rewarding group activity. Use it as an opportunity to get to know your neighbors if you don't already and to strengthen existing neighborly bonds. The following suggestions for tree preservation range from low-level group investment to broader community involvement and advocacy.

Adopt a tree. Get a few of your neighbors to individually or collectively adopt a tree and commit to doing the tree maintenance tasks discussed above. Start a text chain or email list to send out reminders for watering trees during droughts or particularly hot weather, keeping tree boxes free of garbage and pet waste, and evaluating tree health in the summer. If you want a more formal setup or you don't want to be your neighborhood's tree maintenance supervisor, you can see if your city has an official tree adoption program. Through these programs, residents can sign up to care for specific trees and receive text reminders to water the trees and clear debris.

If you're not much of a talker (I'm married to one) or aren't ready to establish an in-person relationship with your neighbors, it's totally fine to contact them in writing. Introduce yourself (giving as little or as much information as you feel comfortable with) and let them know why you're reaching out and how to contact you. Short on time? Here's an example template that you can type up and pop into neighbors' mailboxes or slip under their doors:

> *Hi!*
>
> *I'm a neighbor on* [**insert street name here**]. *There are several trees on our street that reduce flooding when it rains, keep the*

neighborhood cool in the summer, and make our block look more beautiful. I'm starting an "adopt-a-tree" program on our block to protect those trees and keep them healthy, and I would love for you to join! Would you be interested in learning more about how to keep the [**describe tree and its location**] *healthy? Adopting a tree is simple: about two or three times a year, I'll send out an email or a text with some tips on how to care for your tree, such as watering it during droughts or clearing trash away from the roots. Three neighbors have already joined—can we count you as the fourth? If so, text me at* [**insert phone number**] *or email me at* [**insert email address**].*

Thanks!

—[**Your name**]

Obviously, don't say that three people have signed on unless it's true. But if it is true, milk that fact! People are more willing to join in when they see others doing the same. When I was trying to get our utility company to fix a gas leak killing the trees in our community, I organized my neighbors to join the fight. But there were a few neighbors I just couldn't get to sign on until they saw that others on the block had joined, even though I already had positive relationships with them.

Neighborhood Tree Walks. If you're up for a bigger role, grab a few folks and lead a walk through your neighborhood a few times per year to take notes on local tree health, clear trash out of tree boxes, and identify areas for tree replacement or the planting of new trees. This activity is great to do with children in your life and can strengthen casual bonds between neighbors. If a curious passerby asks what you're up to, let them know you live in the neighborhood and are looking out for the trees to help reduce flooding and heat. Recommend that they water their trees during hot weather and clear out garbage whenever they see it. If they want to do more, offer to add them to the tree-care text chain or connect them to your community's adopt-a-tree program (if it exists).

Voice your concerns to your city councilor and to those who sit on committees in charge of land development. I'm not saying to dust off your picket signs and block all new development that would harm trees (but you can do that, too, if you're into it). Communities need housing, stores, cycle tracks, bus lanes, and all sorts of development to meet the needs of people who live there. What I *am* saying is to take advantage of your opportunity to speak up through public hearings and **ask for smart development** that recognizes the contributions that trees make, cooling neighborhoods and protecting against floods. Increasingly, municipalities are reframing trees as public infrastructure akin to roads, streetlights, and sidewalks. If the community is currently benefiting from trees as infrastructure, all parties should be taking their removal and replacement as seriously as removing a road or paving over a park.

When I think of the small and spindly sapling planted outside our apartment, I tend to think of its care through the eyes of my five-year-old daughter. By the time she's my age, she'll be facing a hotter, wetter, more unpredictable future, but for now, she's contributing to making a sliver of the city a little cooler, drier, and more pleasant. She helps me drag a bucket and a hose out to the sidewalk on hot days to siphon water into the tree bag. She wears tiny, blue padded gardening gloves to help me empty the tree box of trash that has blown down our block. These relatively small actions can be done just as well quickly and on the go or with the slow focus of learning to care for something new; no matter how you do it, just the act of doing is a gift to those here now—and those yet to come.

These small acts can be empowering, dispelling feelings that change is too complex or too hard to come by and replacing them with a sense of ownership over the built environment and our collective future. If the ideas laid out in these first few chapters resonate with you and feel doable, that's a great place to start. But not all the interventions you might want to see are fully within your locus of control. As discussed in chapter one, our communities look the way they do for a reason. Human beings, sometimes as far back as a century ago, made decisions about the way resources were distributed, and those historical decisions have real, contemporary impacts on how we experience the climate crisis. To keep our communities safer from heat, flood, and fire, we need to engage with, modify, or upend those decisions. The following chapters focus on the next steps to lasting change: impacting how decisions are made and resources distributed in your municipality.

CHAPTER 4

The Three Questions

WHEN YOU'RE LOOKING AROUND your community asking key questions about the way your built environment handles heat, fire, and water, you may wonder, if these changes were important, wouldn't they have happened already? If we've long been aware of inequity, of unfairness, of tangible harm, if we've long known that we need green infrastructure to lower temperatures and stem flooding, why hasn't change already come about?

Before we dig into that question and begin to sketch out how you can organize for collective action, I'd like to talk about your responsibility as someone actively seeking to shape the world into something that is fairer, wiser, and more stable than what you're likely pushing up against. When thinking about this topic, I like to consider the famous questions posed by first-century religious scholar Rabbi Hillel:

> *If I am not for myself, who will be for me?*
> *If I am only for myself, what am I?*
> *And if not now, when?*   —Rabbi Hillel the Elder[1]

This quote, which my mother, an early childhood educator, kept taped to the refrigerator in my childhood home, teases out our human responsibility to ourselves and to one another. We have a responsibility to speak up for and protect ourselves *and* a deep responsibility to use our knowledge, power, and energy to advocate alongside others. I'm not recommending you find a new neighborhood and launch climate action work *on behalf* of others; rather, I'm recommending you do this work *in partnership* with others. The difference is important.

A large part of climate justice work is fixing the harm that has occurred by pulling up pavement and planting trees, but an equally important component is preventing similar harm from happening again by modifying the structures and systems that have caused these issues, made change slow and painfully hard to come by, and excluded those most at risk from decision-making processes. Those closest to the problem have a uniquely rich knowledge and understanding of what is necessary, and it's a knowledge that can't be replaced by any professional expert or text (including this one)!

Low-income communities and communities of color are woefully familiar with organizations, institutions, and individuals parachuting in with "solutions" that, although they may be well-intentioned, are deeply divorced from the reality on the ground. When you're working on issues that directly affect you, you're the expert, but as you seek to help others, remember to connect with those who are most impacted and prioritize their voices and expertise. Don't assume you know what they want or what they need.

Conversely, if you're in one of those communities where well-meaning individuals or organizations from outside the community are trying to make change without your guidance and leadership, you have both the right and the responsibility to push back. What you know, what you're concerned about, what questions you have all matter. The most powerful way to be included is to show up. In Los Angeles, a citywide organization dedicated to greenspaces came up with a plan to turn a contaminated parcel of land in the southeast portion of the city into a community asset, providing stormwater retention, heat reduction, and open space for children to play—the site was going to meet so many challenges identified through maps and models. However, the engagement process with residents was limited. Residents hadn't been properly informed about the cleanup and development process and had more questions than answers about the possibility of machines kicking up contaminated soil so close to their homes. When bulldozers arrived to begin remediation, locals were there to block them and demand more thorough community engagement. Residents were successful in pausing the process, and the organization responded well, hiring members of the community to liaise, hosting Spanish-first meetings (then translated into English), and engaging with residents where they were most likely to be found instead of expecting them to travel to a formal meeting. If your neighborhood is similarly facing neglect or changes that haven't taken community expertise into account, never underestimate the collective power you can exercise by showing up and speaking out with others.

Collective power is key to stable, wise, lasting change. As we will discuss in future chapters, local governments and institutions have limited attention, and what resources they have are pulled in an astounding number of directions. To get on their radar and prioritize the changes you see as key to your neighborhood's security, you'll have to elevate your concerns and ideas, and that's most effectively done with others who can lend their experience, expertise, and person-power to the process.

There are challenges when you bring people together to advocate for climate resilience. It's common to run into people or groups who reject the label of "environmentalist," and you might not see yourself as one either, there's a fair reason for that. Mainstream environmentalism in our culture has a tough rap, in part because its focus has for so long been on natural systems that are out of view for the majority of people, embedded deep in the woods of the West or in far-off locations like the Arctic. While Black, Brown, Indigenous, and low-income communities have, since time immemorial, organized to steward built and natural environments in nearly every corner of the planet, in dominant American culture, the image of an "environmentalist" tends to be a White dude in a quarter-zip Patagonia fleece staring out at a mountain vista. Some of this imagery comes from outdoor recreation companies wanting to sell pricey jackets and tents to people with lots of disposable income. But the marketing campaigns are drawing from a history of American conservation that explicitly and intentionally limited the outdoors as White spaces and framed the environment as something that needs to be kept "pristine" and "protected," often at the expense of Indigenous, Black, and Brown people. This perspective in conservation lacks nuance because it neglects the reality that we all have historically had an active role to play in conservation.

Compared to many other countries, the United States is unique in the sheer amount of protected public land it has in the form of state and national parks and forests. Former president Theodore Roosevelt, considered by many to be one of the founders of the conservationist movement in the United States, viewed wild spaces as the inheritance of generations yet unborn and implored Americans to "leave it as it is. You cannot improve on it.... What you can do is to keep it for your children, your children's children, and for all who come after you."[2] But, by annexing nearly 86 million acres of tribal land into the national forest system, thereby displacing the Indigenous people who had carefully stewarded it for thousands of years, Roosevelt made it clear that the parks were actually for *White* generations yet unborn.[3] From John Muir, renowned conservationist and founder of the Sierra Club, to Madison Grant, founder of the famed Bronx Zoo, conservationists and their adjacent institutions saw the environment as a set of resources to be set aside for White, aristocratic men to govern and then visit when in need of recharging.[4]

Environmentalists and conservationists have traditionally projected values that prioritize a western, manifest destiny–style dominion over the land and over the needs of the people who have historically lived there. In an 1886 lecture called "Ranch Life in the West," Roosevelt wrote, "I don't go so far as to think that the only good Indian is the dead Indian, but I believe nine out of every ten are, and I shouldn't like to inquire too closely into the case of the tenth. The most vicious cowboy has more moral principle than the average Indian." With such despicable and racist values at heart of the conservation movement, it is no surprise that in the intervening centuries, western scientific methods have been prioritized over the knowledge of the Indigenous people who hold generations of expertise in caring for their ancestral lands. It is only in the past few decades that indigenous methods such as prescribed burning as a means of preventing more damaging and uncontrollable fires are making their way into the forestry mainstream.

The complex history of conservation has impacted what mainstream environmentalism has focused on and has shaped the conversation about the impacts of the climate to prioritize wild spaces over more populated areas. There is certainly a great deal to pay attention to outside of our cities. In 2021, the Arctic slammed into the headlines for reaching, at time of writing, its highest ever recorded temperature, 100.4°F. The national conversation centered around collapsing ice sheets, thawing permafrost, and ice melting so quickly that polar bears, which can swim between 50 and 400 contiguous miles, were getting stranded between ice floes and drowning at sea. In 2022, one billion snow crabs disappeared from the floor of the Bering Sea—90 percent of the population— likely due to back-to-back years of slightly elevated water temperatures that melted sea ice, increased the crabs' metabolic needs, and reduced their foraging area.[5] For many, this news was absolutely terrifying, but for others, it was deeply disconnected from the day-to-day experiences of those living in urban environments under the specter of the climate crisis. Land conservation and the preservation of animals is vital to our survival, but environment-centered conversations sometimes forget that our cities and towns *are* environmental systems in their own right and are deserving of as much attention as the plight of the polar bear.

As we saw in chapter three, you have the ability to change the built environment. Planting and maintaining trees, installing rain barrels, cleaning out catch basins—there are countless hyperlocal interventions you can stage that will keep your community safer from the consequences of the climate crisis. But when needs get bigger—say fixing a sapling-smothering gas leak or adding shade structures to a bus route—direct action can rest firmly outside of your locus of control and in the hands of other people and institutions. Sometimes effecting change in the built environment rests with elected officials, city employees, or the private sector—all entities that are part of large, often confusing systems that require a diversity of knowledge and input to change. When engaging with these systems, you cannot and should not stand alone. Heat, flood, drought, fire: these issues often impact the quality of life of multiple people in a community. If, for example, you suffer from persistent basement flooding, your city councilor or planning department will likely consider that a *"you* problem" if you bring your specific situation up to them (assuming you can get their attention at all). At best they might recommend you install a French drain and divert your downspout away from your home. However, if it turns out that basement flooding is a chronic challenge for thirty of the forty homes on your street, that's possibly a municipal drainage issue that is more likely to grab the attention of the local urban planner.

Effecting change requires you to construct a coalition composed of the right people, build an understanding of the change that's required to repair the existing harm and prevent that harm from happening again, and develop a clear-eyed view of the barriers to that change. A part of my paid work is helping residents across the country build the capacity to self-advocate for more climate adaptation resources from their local government. When the teams I work with begin to lend our efforts to community concerns, we spend a fair amount of time wrestling with three key questions that you should ask yourself when you're looking to effect systems change in your community:

1. Who are my people?
2. What is the change they need?
3. Why has that change not yet come about?

These three questions, first introduced to me in a course taught by community organizer and Harvard professor Marshall Ganz, reflect the human responsibility and urgency posed by Rabbi Hillel the Elder's famed questions and give us a framework for gathering the ingredients to effect lasting change.[6]

Who Are My People?

Your people are those who are most impacted by the issue and whose buy-in, participation, and support you will need to change the way resources are distributed and decisions are made. Sometimes it's clear who is most impacted by an issue. In San Diego, California, Chollas Creek cuts through the south-central portion of the city. For years, the creek, which has been channelized[7] in some portions and neglected in others, has erratically and unpredictably overflowed into backyards and homes of the predominantly lower-income Black and Brown families that live nearby. Those people, the ones whose homes and yards have flooded but have limited access to the creek for recreation purposes, would be "your people."

The people who are regularly forced to confront things like flooded roads or roasting hot commutes to work have valuable information regarding the impact of the problem, which is important to communicate to decision makers. They also have strong ideas for interventions that would make that problem bearable. But when the issue is big, it can be hard to narrow down the "who" to a manageable and precise list. You can find out who is most impacted by the problem in a few different ways.

One tool I use is called "five types of capital." This framework creates categories for the things of value we find in the built, natural, and social worlds. They are:

1. Natural capital (the resources we have on Earth that are key to survival, such as water, air, food, and land)
2. Human capital (our skills and livelihood)
3. Social capital (access to institutions, community, and culture, such as schools, museums, and churches)

4. Built capital (the resources that we access to make our day-to-day function, such as public transportation, homes, and cars)
5. Financial capital (money and our ability to access it)

If you were concerned that the local schools were too hot in the spring and fall due to a lack of air conditioning, you'd find your "who" by considering who is impacted by the school closures or extreme heat conditions. When considering **human capital**, you might choose to speak with teachers and custodial staff who are unable to effectively do their work if the building is too hot or they're kept from it entirely. Students who are depending on the institution of school for learning, socialization, and sometimes food may experience disruptions in their access to **social capital** during extreme heat events. Caregivers, such as parents or guardians who work outside the home, might have their **financial capital** impacted if they are forced to take days off of work due to their children's school being canceled. Not every challenge you encounter will intersect with all five types of capital, but it's a useful framework to build your list of stakeholders and help you avoid potential blind spots.

Another method for finding those who are closest to the issue is by contacting organizations or advocacy groups actively working on similar issues to see if what you're concerned about has already been flagged by someone and is being addressed. There's no need to reinvent the wheel when it comes to this work; it's perfectly fine to join groups that are focused on an issue you're interested in and draw their attention to your specific concern. Finding local advocacy groups can be somewhat difficult because they're usually small, often volunteer run, and don't have the time or budgets for things like advertising or self-promotion. Most advocacy groups, however, have some type of relationship with their city or town councilor, so it's usually a good idea to start by asking your elected official to direct you to people already working on the issue.

Similarly, many cities, towns, and even neighborhoods have online communities on platforms such as Facebook. Making a "seeking" post for people who are either concerned about the issue or who know of groups already working on the issue can be a helpful jumping-off point. Note that the people who utilize online platforms are often not thorough and representative cross sections of the community, so sites like Nextdoor, Reddit, and Facebook shouldn't be considered exhaustive by *any* means.

What Is the Change They Need?

The change you and your people need depends on which climate risk poses the most immediate threat and how that threat affects people. The change should be defined by or in consultation with those most impacted. When Chollas Creek in San Diego floods, sewage bubbles up from the storm drains, and children's toys are unexpectedly snatched from backyards. Upstream is a common dumping ground for mattresses, broken appliances, and construction waste. The refuse acts as a dam, causing portions of the creek to overflow, sweeping away residents' patio furniture, and depositing waste at their back doors. For decades, a broad coalition of residents and local people-centered organizations such as churches, neighborhood associations, and nonprofits that were intimately familiar with the seasonal challenges of living so close to the creek clearly articulated their needs: a cleanup of the tons of household and commercial trash in the creek, a dechannelization of the creek bed, and infrastructure improvements to both reduce flooding and improve recreational access. The change they'd like to see was identified through their lived experience of living alongside and observing the creek, hosting exploratory field trips to the creek with fellow advocates and experts, and residents passing on and piecing together generations of community knowledge about the flow of water.

Why Has That Change Not Yet Come About?

All the interventions listed above in San Diego require money, but access to state and federal funding to complete these improvements was off-limits until the city officially recognized the creek as municipal infrastructure. What residents of this formerly redlined area needed was less flooding from and better access to the creek. A major barrier to achieving that need was the lack of access to state and federal resources required to pay for those changes. Change had not yet come about because the creek was not recognized as infrastructure by the City of San Diego.

A broad coalition of stakeholders, including Groundwork San Diego, churches, and neighborhood associations, were successful in persuading the city council, via testimony and field trips with government officials to the creek and surrounding area, to reclassify the creek, opening it up for further funding and repairs.

The three key questions above can be used to build out a valuable infrastructure for understanding who you need to engage with about what to get where. In the next few chapters, we'll dig into how to apply all this information to making change in or around your community. Although I present the steps needed to effect change in a linear fashion for the sake of clarity, nothing about this process is truly linear; you should expect to sometimes be catapulted back to square one due to changes in administration, community priorities, or unpredictable events (for example, a deadly pandemic). Changing how resources are distributed or who gets to make decisions involves twists and turns and unexpected happenings. People move out of the neighborhood, priorities change, and elections happen, which might require you to find more information, get in contact with a new expert, or change your approach. A normal, well-functioning process can be quick or lengthy, discouraging or energizing, straightforward or convoluted; all are normal. Once you have the building blocks of how to find the right information, who to work with, and what to ask, you'll be in good shape to weather whatever comes your way.

CHAPTER 5

Experts, Allies, and Naysayers

BEFORE OUR DAUGHTER ENTERED ELEMENTARY SCHOOL, we'd bike her to a daycare center over the city line, closer to our jobs. During the summer, the first leg of cycling was always miserable and hot. While motorists idled in their air-conditioned cars and trucks, I would wait at a stoplight in the bike lane, dripping with sweat under the rising summer sun. On the sidewalk to my right, damp commuters trudged to the bus and subway lines, the only shade a few thin rectangles cast by the desiccated trunks of dead, leafless trees.

A half mile from our home, in the adjoining city, the closed canopy of mature trees cooled the streets enough to slow my sweat, cut the glare from the sun, and freshen the air. Each day as I coasted into the shade, I wondered why the trees were able to thrive here, but just across the city line near our home, you could walk nearly a quarter mile from our door before you would touch a living tree. After two months of brutal, sweat-soaked daycare drop-offs, I started looking into who oversees the street trees and why they had yet to be replanted. Our city is lucky enough to have an urban forester, so I reached out, asking if she planned to do a replanting and if so, when. She replied with the facts: the trees had been dead for about six years, the roots smothered by the slow release of methane from a natural gas leak detected by the city. Any trees planted in that soil would die, and the city (understandably) would not consider replacing them until the leak was fixed. The city had no power to directly compel the gas company to repair the leaks in absence of an explosion risk—the threshold of which was dictated by state law. Legislation in my state accepts methane leaks (which hasten global warming and destroy municipal green infrastructure) as an acceptable cost of transporting natural gas to people's homes. If I wanted tree canopy cover on that street, I was going to have to figure out how to get around these obstacles. I didn't know enough about how my local government or the utilities worked to individually address this problem, so I knew I needed to look beyond the individual solutions I was used to employing and find others to work with. I needed experts who could share their knowledge and allies who were willing to learn alongside me, lending their own skills and energy to the mix.

The Second "Who"

Let's talk a little bit more about the "who" when it comes to effecting change at the local level, because there are actually two "who's" to consider. We've covered the first—those who are closest to the issue. Connecting with those who are impacted by the problem is an important pathway to finding a solution that effectively addresses that challenge. The second "who" are those who may or may not be intimately familiar with the issue but are moved to help you effect change by lending their unique knowledge of subjects and systems (experts), their broad skills and presence (allies), or their skepticism (naysayers). Those closest to the issue form the foundation of your people, but that group isn't guaranteed to be large enough to effectively share the work or to have the time, expertise, or energy needed to contribute to lasting change. For that, you need to pull in experts, allies, and naysayers.

Experts are those people who have some niche subject-matter knowledge or skill that fills gaps in your coalition—everyone from a council member who knows the administrative process through and through to a gardener who knows their way around water drainage. One of the many reasons to seek a variety of expertise in your coalition is that your local government doesn't and can't know everything. You can't rely on your city councilors or even municipal employees to have *all* the detailed knowledge required to understand and solve a problem. Experts help close knowledge gaps in both your coalition and your local government.

Allies are folks who might not have lots of extra time, money, or expertise, but are generally supportive of your ideas and willing to lend their name, skills (such as writing, relationship building, or public speaking), and attention to the cause by attending community meetings, signing open letters, or collecting community data.

Naysayers think your concerns and proposed solutions are overblown, underdeveloped, or impractical, but their arguments can help strengthen your own by forcing you to defend your position.

How to Find Them

Although you can accomplish much by yourself, this work is a heck of a lot easier and more fun to approach as a group effort. There's data to be collected, decision makers to be contacted, and strategies to be developed and executed, and that's a lot to rest on the shoulders of a single individual. You might be the first person to tackle your specific concern in your specific location, but there are others nearby who know something about the systems with which you need to interact, have dealt with those systems themselves, or have specialized knowledge that might take a long time for you to develop. Inviting experts, allies, and naysayers into your work allows you to speed up the learning process, make more effective and efficient decisions, and prevent burnout in what might realistically be a lengthy process.

You can find your experts, allies, and naysayers by using channels similar to those used for finding those closest to an issue. City councilors, organizations, or advocacy groups working on adjacent issues are great places to start, but friends, colleagues, and relations will also connect you to who you need to meet. When I was running in circles trying to get the gas company and city officials to fix the leak, I happened to mention the issue to my then boss, who reminded me about Mothers Out Front, a national nonprofit with local volunteer-based chapters that have led effective gas leak repair campaigns nationwide over the past few years. I needed the gas leaks to be repaired, so this group was as good a lead as any to follow. When I reached out by email, it turned out that Randi, the leader of the local chapter, not only worked on a similar campaign across the city but also lived a few blocks away from me and had deep roots in our neighborhood.

Randi has lived in her home for about fifteen years, and her two kids attend the local elementary and high schools. She is an active Boy Scouts mom, volunteers at community events, and is the kind of reliable, thoughtful person you would flag down if you were in a pickle. She's capable, curious, and has an exceptionally large mental Rolodex. Hanging out with Randi at a café is notoriously difficult because you are likely to be interrupted two to three times an hour by passersby who want to breathlessly update her on everything from an article they just read to gifts they picked up for their grandkids. Randi knows the neighborhood and the people who work for and live in the city, and if there's something or someone she doesn't know, she likely knows who does. Randi has a special type of expertise because of the depth and breadth at which she knows people and systems—Randi is a "community connector."

When the gas company denied that there was a leak along the corridor, Randi remembered a successful gas leak repair campaign led across town a few years earlier. She connected me to the residents who'd led the charge, and one week later, on a chilly October afternoon, I was walking the corridor with them talking strategy: who in city council to partner with, what types of data we would need to collect (beyond a count of the dead trees and the location of foul odors) to sway decision makers, and how to get others on board to lend their expertise, their support, and their skepticism.

If you are new to town, live in a big neighborhood with a lot of turnover, or have just been busy with your own life, it might be challenging to find your Randi or the handful of Randis who collectively hold the information and relationships you need. You can start your search by looking for local people or groups working on issues that you care about who can act as community connectors and introduce you to the experts, allies, and naysayers who will help your cause.

People who are involved in community improvement efforts have already gone through the work of building relationships and learning who's who in local government and have a sense of the various allies who are willing to join organized efforts. Once you find them, invite these people out for coffee or to hop on the phone. Use this meeting as a chance to ask about their work, to seek out their thoughts on how to effect change at the local level, and to tell them what you are trying to do. In my personal and professional experience, I have found that if you ask politely and are flexible with when to meet, people are very generous with their time and expertise. They *want* to share what they have done and to lend their know-how. Having a chance to tell their stories, share their opinions, and offer advice is a joyful and energizing experience for most people. At the end of the conversation, ask if there are others they think you should talk to or if they know of other allies who might be interested in joining you.

It's likely that somewhere near you there's a nonprofit, community group, or organization already focusing on climate adaptation, watershed management, or tree planting—connect with them to learn more about their work and how you can support their efforts. WE ACT in New York City, Green Roots in Chelsea, Massachusetts, and Little Manila Rising in Stockton, California, are all great examples of organizations working to green, clean, and protect their communities. Informal groups such as neighborhood associations and community coalitions often interface with both the municipality and local nonprofits and are led by volunteers. Again, search engines can be really helpful here in finding groups that work on issues similar to your own. Note that the groups you are interested in might be so small that they don't have websites, so make sure to review any local news stories (both articles and videos) that pop up. They will often have interviews with residents and coalitions who are making change at the neighborhood level but might not have a high public profile. Also look for these groups tabling at community events such as festivals, civic events, parades, and farmers' markets.

It's common for cities and towns to have advisory committees tasked by the municipality with providing guidance on environmental issues. One of the first group of experts we pulled into the gas leaks discussion was the city's urban forestry committee.[1]

Composed of tree experts, engineers, and committed tree conser-vationists, our urban forestry committee serves as a link between city departments and the public, making recommendations on ur-ban forestry strategy, outreach, and stewardship. Finding relevant committees in your community can be a way of furthering your understanding of local priorities.

Roles of the Constituency

Pulling together those who are impacted alongside your experts, allies, and naysayers is called building a coalition or constituency, a group of supporters who are standing together for a common cause. Working with your constituency will not only give you wise ideas and a bank of skills, but its size and diversity will also make your cause appear urgent to decision makers. A single person is easy to ignore, but a group increases officials' perceptions that the issue is important and should be considered. The size of your co-alition will vary a lot by the size of your community. To draw attention in, say, Los Angeles, you'll need a bigger group than you would in, say, Paris, Kentucky.

You should note, however, that not everyone who is part of your coalition needs to be doing everything all the time, and you should use people's time judiciously to avoid exhaustion. When signing petitions or open letters or holding a protest to which you've in-vited the media, for example, as many people as you can get on board, the better. But if you're giving a presentation at a town meeting or taking your city forester on a field trip of your neigh-borhood to experience the low canopy cover, it's not necessary to get everyone to show up; in those cases, bringing along one or two people from each category (a person closest to the issue, an expert, an ally, a naysayer) can be helpful in keeping the experi-ence and conversation focused and manageable. During smaller and more intimate events, those closest to the issue are able to talk about the human impact and frame out the solutions that would best mitigate the challenge. Experts can add nuance and detail while fleshing out the path to operationalizing suggestions, but, in order to avoid infighting or experts assuming disproportionate leadership, be sure that experts brought into the conversation are on board with prioritizing the change that those closest to the problem would like to see. Agreeing on talking points and overall messaging is important before engaging an expert in public-facing dialogues. Allies are there to learn, to ask novice questions that further discussion, and ultimately to report back to the group and celebrate successes. But what about the naysayer?

It might seem counterintuitive to bring someone who is skeptical of your work into the picture, but their presence is invaluable. On a field trip to the treeless avenue in my community, I was accompanied by a city councilor from the infrastructure committee (an administrative expert), a member of the urban forestry commission (a regulations and tree expert), a representative from the gas company, members of our local chapter of Mothers Out Front (allies), and a very skeptical civil engineer from the neighborhood who tried at every turn to poke holes in the argument that gas leaks were responsible for the tree loss (the naysayer). His skepticism unearthed questions and concerns that likely would have arisen at some point. Having the engineer dig at the problem from every angle gave us an opportunity to collectively engage in rich, data-informed discussions at the site, saving us time and effort later. You won't always sway your naysayers, but if you can convince them of your ideas, they can offer added credibility. In our case, we were surprised when the engineer spoke passionately about the value of trees at the next city council meeting on gas leaks. He brought a new framing to the discussion during his powerful testimony by describing the trees as vital infrastructure, "as important as roads and bridges," and implored the city council to find a way to require the gas company to fix the leaks.

Allies, experts, and community connectors can usually help you find your naysayer by identifying members of the community or municipality who have historically opposed, been skeptical of, or spoken out against similar issues. Also, the more public your quest to build a coalition, the more likely it is that you'll naturally run into naysayers embedded in the community. If all else fails, most people know someone who just knows how to ask really good questions and is able to play devil's advocate. Note that your naysayer doesn't have to be contentious or vehemently against your issue to be valuable to your cause. You're looking for someone who sees the other side of the issue and is good at asking difficult questions and probing for answers.

You've Gotta Talk

Regardless of what group you're looking to connect with, if you want to move the needle on change at the local level, you'll need to talk to people. The dominant American culture is one that is friendly but not always intimate, and perhaps the idea of approaching your friends and neighbors, let alone strangers, to ask for their time or help seems scary. I promise it's worth the effort. I'll admit that I'm a relatively chatty person. I like striking up conversations with the clerk at the post office and asking taxi drivers what they love (and hate!) about their city. But even I don't like talking to strangers if I have to ask them for something or if I expect they will ask me for something I do not feel comfortable agreeing to on the spot.

I'm not looking to frighten shy folks by suggesting you need to stand on a corner with a clipboard intercepting folks as they pass by (though that is an option), but you will need to communicate with others to connect about a climate issue, get more information about what the issue is and how it is impacting others, and unearth the history behind why this problem even exists in the first place. The good news is that when you connect with others about your shared community, most people are eager to engage. It's hard to know how you feel about a random international charity fund-raising in front of the supermarket (Are they reputable? How do they spend their funding? Can I afford a monthly donation in this economy? How *do* I feel about this issue?), but you'd probably respond differently if someone you know, even in passing, asked for your opinion about getting trees planted near the local library or the intersection by your house. Even my spouse, a quiet person who would rather not strike up a conversation with a stranger, is happy to lend a hand or answer a question if the ask is clear, direct, and in line with his interests. Generally, people want to help others. That's why you're holding this book!

Teachers are fond of noting that there are no stupid questions; if you're curious about something, someone else probably is, too. I think that belief is also transferable to advocacy issues. However big or small the local challenge is, it's very likely someone else is also curious about it and is eager to contribute their energy and talents to making change. You just need to find them.

You don't have to start talking to strangers right away. It's easiest to start with people you know, either your primary relationships—family members, friends, coworkers—or your secondary relationships—people you know casually from repeated interactions at places like cafés, sports clubs, or local institutions such as schools, places of worship, and online groups. It's similar to approaching neighbors and friends about caring for neighborhood trees.

If you already have a deep relationship with those in your

community or if you're gregarious enough to chat with strangers, start by asking questions. Regardless of who you start with, you should be clear from the jump about why you are talking to them and what you want.

For example:

- To the barista or a café patron: "I noticed that it's really hot in front of this café! Do you know if this block used to have trees?"
- To a parent: "I think our kids go to the same school, and it looks like you walk a similar route. Did you notice that the crosswalk on Elm Street keeps flooding when it rains?"
- To your neighbor: "Hi [neighbor]! When the commuter rail passes by, we've been getting a lot of diesel smoke coming in through our window. Does the same happen to you, too?"

In these example conversations, you're looking to build historical knowledge, understand how people view the issue you are concerned about, and develop relationships that will come in handy later. Let the conversation take you where it will. This person might have noticed the same things you did and have more information or might be interested in getting involved; if so, it's a good chance to ask if they'd like to stay connected. For example: "It's been great talking to you about this issue. I'm looking to get some residents together to fix it. Can I get your email to keep you updated and check in with you about it later?" If they say yes, great! If they say no, that's fine, too! Don't pester. It is also possible that some of the people you approach might not be interested in chatting, have no information, or may have never noticed the problem you're pointing out. That's okay, too! Be pleasant and check in with someone else. Remember that it can take a while for trust and relationships to build. The individuals you connect with might not, at first touch, think that change is possible or that your idea could be part of achieving that change. Leave the door open to those who seem lukewarm or disinterested. They may decide to join in later.

If chatting up folks in public is not your style, you are pressed for time, or you have restrictions or disabilities that make in-person communication a challenge, the digital realm is a great option. Email, video chat, and phone are all fine and great time-savers. You can connect via emailing a neighborhood association listserv or posting where locals might be able to see it, such as a community-specific Facebook group. We are simultaneously blessed and cursed when it comes to the internet. It is easier than ever to connect with people who share common interests, but online community platforms such as Facebook, Nextdoor, and Reddit are complicated. They have well-earned reputations for being both great spots for community building *and* noxious playgrounds for racist, classist, xenophobic, or grouchy people to say horrible things to strangers and shake their fists at community progress. That said, groups that sit at the overlap between hyperspecific locations (we are talking neighborhood level as compared to city- or statewide) and specific activities such as gardening, parenting, mutual aid, and climate activism are intimate enough that the kind of garbage the internet is known for doesn't happen as frequently as in other groups. It is harder to be rude to someone online when you have a good chance of running into that person at the hardware store.

"Does Anybody Care?"

When you speak with people about community-specific topics, be prepared to encounter exhaustion on the part of residents closest to the issue. If they are aware of the issue, it's likely they have had to endure this problem for years or decades and might, understandably, feel that change isn't possible.

In the Oakgrove-Bellemeade neighborhood of Richmond, Virginia, a majority-Black community, crosswalks and intersections are quickly underwater after a summer rain. "Out West, there isn't enough water; here in Richmond, Virginia, we're covered in it," says Rob Jones, executive director of Groundwork RVA, a local youth workforce and environmental justice nonprofit. When the road was dry, residents were also concerned about the day-to-day risk posed by speeding cars. The straight, open boulevard and lack of stop signs encouraged speeding, and just about everyone felt unsafe as they tried to cross. Residents had strong opinions (and excellent ideas, including planting trees to both calm traffic and absorb water) about how their own flooding intersections could be improved, but they said they believed that there was no way change would come about. "We've been calling for years, and no one does anything for us. They're not going to do anything," noted a senior resident. Community members found themselves trapped in an everlasting game of municipal musical chairs. Melissa Guevara, a community organizer and youth program director at Groundwork RVA, relayed stories of residents calling municipal departments and being put on hold endlessly. They'd be transferred from one department to another until they were transferred back to the person who had initially answered their call. Automated phone trees would land them at voicemails too full to take additional messages. If by some miracle they *did* make it through to a person, their requests would be dutifully noted by someone on the other end of the line, but year after year, no traffic calming or flood reduction interventions would appear. There was a deep feeling of mistrust and disbelief among residents that the local government shared any interest in the neighborhood.

In my community, when I spoke to some neighbors about the dead trees and leaking gas, many shrugged. Most neighbors I connected with liked the idea of a greener corridor, but many avoided walking, choosing to use their cars for short trips to the grocery store rather than endure the heat beating down on them and choking car exhaust on that stretch of the road. Long-term residents noted that the area had smelled of gas for years, and they expected it never would change. Mary, a neighborhood resident of more than fifty years whose home is closest to the leaks, told me that she'd been calling the gas company regularly for a decade about the persistent smell of methane outside her building. "The gas company doesn't care! The city doesn't care! And no one else will call when they smell it. They just pass on by. It stinks out here and no one cares." While supportive of my goals to fix the leak and replant the street, even my husband was skeptical that anything could be done. He didn't believe that this fight was winnable—if this street were a priority, it would have been dealt with already.

Part of overcoming skepticism is building relationships with others, which is a slow process. When you show that you care, that you're listening to and invested in others' concerns, you'll start to build trust. As you make progress, be sure to update those in your community. If skeptics see you plugging away at the challenge, launching individual solutions, and keeping the issue at top of mind, you'll eventually break through their belief that change isn't possible and earn their trust on the issue.

Connect for the Long Haul

Remember that climate justice work is about making change for the long haul. Change, and accountability for maintaining that change, can only remain stable and lasting if it rests on the shoulders of a group of people—people who can take over when someone needs to take a break or shift their attention to a sick family member or new baby, share institutional knowledge so that it's not lost, and bring their unique skills and perspective to the work. Additionally, it makes the workload significantly more manageable if everyone can take over in their areas of strength or skills. Strong writers can pen petitions, open letters, and op-eds to draw attention to your efforts, strong facilitators can lead meetings, artists can design eye-catching posters advertising the next data-gathering event, and so on.

This work is also a good opportunity to build community. A defining characteristic of American culture is that we're a lonely people. Around 35 percent of American adults report feelings of *serious* loneliness, and that number increases to 61 percent for young adults.[2] We're busy, spread out, stressed out, and doing our best to make ends meet. In cities and suburbs alike, it's increasingly difficult to find places to congregate and connect with others that don't require spending money. While you might not find your next best friend or lover organizing for local change, working toward impacting your community can give you a sense of shared purpose with others and increases the likelihood you'll end up engaging in repeated, small, casual interactions around town that result in feeling like part of a community. And it's that community that will make launching future actions faster, easier, and more joyful.

CHAPTER 6

Who's in Charge around Here?

SOMETIMES THE PATH TO CHANGE requires action from your local government, so it helps to have a solid understanding of how decisions about the built environment are made, who gets to make them, and where the opportunities for intervention lie. Your local government directly controls substantial portions of the built environment and enforces the rules and regulations that apply to private entities. Although occupying a powerful space in the community, outside of calling 311 to report a pothole or uncollected trash, the average person has minimal experience reaching out to their municipality.[1] Local governments can be opaque, and it's not always easy to know where to start, who to talk to, or what to say to get their attention and partnership. But lasting, stable change isn't going to come about without regulation and policy. So, who makes up your local government, and how do you get their attention?

Mayor versus Councilor

Your mayor represents the entirety of the city, while the councilors (also called alderperson, commissioner, selectperson, or trustee, depending on the community) represent specific neighborhoods, districts, or wards within the municipality.[2] You vote for both mayor and councilor in your local elections. In a "strong mayor" municipality, the mayor acts similarly to the US president in that they set policy agendas, sign off on legislation passed by the council, and have administrative authority to appoint and dismiss the heads of departments. In a "weak mayor" municipality, the mayor has little formal authority outside of their role as the chair of the council, and many day-to-day administrative duties are carried out by an appointed role called the "city/town manager" or, in some cases, are split between the mayor and members of the city council. This isn't a firm rule, but if you live in a major city in your state— think Santa Fe, New Mexico, or Cleveland, Ohio—you likely live in a "strong mayor" community. If you live in a smaller city or town, such as Cambridge, Massachusetts, or Plainview, Texas, there's a good chance your system is a "weak mayor" system. Some communities have a hybrid system. In recent years, many "weak mayor" communities have sought to centralize authority and transition to a "strong mayor" system.

Unless you live in a very small community, talking to the mayor or the city manager about an issue isn't a particularly helpful first step—if you can even get an audience in the first place. I live in a small city with a strong mayor system. Our mayor is constantly on the move, attending everything from regional meetings to ribbon-cutting ceremonies for public projects. Sometimes, it's possible to catch her briefly over the snack table at the start of a community event. But generally, mayors and city managers aren't able to give you the face-to-face time and attention you need to make progress on an issue unless you've arrived with a coalition of allies and stakeholders to grab their attention.

If you're looking to raise an issue, understand the government's priorities, and learn more about pathways to change, you should start with your council person. Councilors are the most direct form of representation you have. They pass local legislation, review and approve the municipality's budget, and usually serve on a variety of committees or subcommittees that study and act on issues such as transportation, housing, utilities, open space, and the environment. With enough public pressure, a city council can also establish specialized subcommittees to review and make progress on short-term issues.

For a while I viewed councilors as beyond my reach. How could I just strike up a conversation with someone whose face was on T-shirts and buttons? It wasn't until I attended my neighbor's de-paving party and spent the afternoon clawing up asphalt beside a city councilor that I realized he was just a regular guy trying his best to avoid a sunburn while prying up a driveway. Your city councilors are your neighbors, and although they may or may not share your values and beliefs, they *are* interested in what's happening in your community. If shared space and place isn't enough to move councilors to connect with you, remember that your vote, and thus your approval, matters tremendously to them because it directly impacts their ability to serve in office. You can find a decent bit of information about councilors online, including which subcommittees they sit on, their email addresses or phone numbers, and social media profiles that they use to communicate with their constituency. When you have a specific issue to raise, and especially as you grow your coalition, reach out to schedule a meeting with them so that they can get to know you and learn more about your concerns and ideas.

City councilors are quite knowledgeable about how various local government agencies function, what the current priorities of the government are, and which committees are addressing which issues. You can reach out to your councilor to better understand who is in charge of a committee or specific municipal project, to see if the issue you care about has already been identified and is being addressed, or to be connected to other organizations or individuals who have unique knowledge or experience working on the issue. You also might request an action from your council, such as for a subcommittee to study a particular issue, intervene in a planning project, or join you for a site visit to better understand your concerns. Take advantage of your local government by pulling councilors in when you need help or information about local history or how local systems function. If your councilor doesn't have their contact information online, you can call the municipality's main line for this information. If you're going to reach out to your councilor, be brief and clear about your request. State up front if you are asking them for information or requesting that they act on an issue.

Don't give up or take it personally if your council member is slow to reply. Although representing the community is a lot of work, it's common for councilors to have other jobs (city council positions tend not to pay well) or commitments. If an issue is urgent, I find it helpful to copy other council members. Occasionally, your councilor may be unfamiliar with the topic you care about, but another councilor may be able to step in with background information or leads on who might be able to help instead. Copying other councilors also applies peer pressure to your elected representative to meet the needs of their constituency.

Mayor and city council seats are elected positions, so you do have considerable leverage to influence their priorities and actions through voting. Voter rates can fluctuate, but turnout for local elections is usually "abysmally low," according to the Who Votes for Mayor? project from Portland State University. Between 2011 and 2015, voter turnout was less than 15 percent in ten of the thirty largest cities in the United States.[3] If you are eligible to vote in your local elections, your vote can potentially carry a lot of power when it comes to who represents you and your needs.

I'm not here to shame you if you don't turn out for local elections—there are significant barriers to voting in the United States. Voting rules vary from place to place, polling times and locations can be inconvenient, and there are often a bunch of positions on the ballot that you've never heard of and don't have time to fully research. I vote in every local election, and I can't even count how many times I've had to look up the role of "comptroller" on my phone while waiting in line to vote. That said, your local government is the body most able to implement rapid change that meets community needs. Your elected officials are in charge of re-distributing the money from federal and state governments and for setting the priorities that municipal employees are charged with carrying out. If you don't vote, there's no guarantee that those elected will share your values and priorities. You need elected officials who are open to pursuing change, and those who are open to pursuing change won't be in office unless you vote for them.

Municipal Departments

Your mayor and councilors are elected officials in charge of the overall direction and oversight of the community, but it's non-elected municipal employees who keep the gears running day to day. These folks are hired or appointed into their positions, and depending on the size of your community, they handle everything from sanitation services to sidewalk repairs to planting street trees, often on a shoestring budget with limited support.

There's usually a person or department in charge of the issue you're interested in, and you can find them through your city's organizational chart, which is often posted online. A city's organizational chart is a helpful visual that captures who is directly in charge of certain departments and positions, and it also shows you how these departments are related to one another. Occasionally, these websites will list the names, email addresses, or phone numbers of departments and their staff, but often you're just left with a name of divisions and positions. Use that information to navigate the phone tree at your local government's central phone number.

It's challenging to give you a guide to organizational charts in this book because the way municipalities order themselves, and the language they use, varies greatly. In general, for climate-related issues, you want to check out the public works, community development, environment, and infrastructure departments, though some cities will also have highly specialized divisions. Phoenix, Arizona, for example, has an Office of Heat Response and Mitigation.

In American culture, there's an unfortunate stereotype of the beleaguered, grouchy municipal employee, but having worked in local government and partnered with municipal employees across the country for years, I can attest that most folks doing this work are pleasant, helpful, and committed to improving their communities. A few polite and kind words are likely to get you what you need. So, how can municipal employees help? They can get you everything from a new street tree on your block to information about public works' priorities to their thoughts on how to get a neighborhood's needs addressed. Municipal staff tend to span political administrations and have one of the best perspectives on how to effect lasting change at the local level. If you're patient, persistent, and friendly, you're likely to build a great partnership with folks who can help you now and over the long haul.

Boards and Commissions

In addition to municipal offices, many cities appoint residents to boards or commissions on specific topics, such as planning, zoning, and urban forestry. These boards and commissions help put decision-making authority into the hands of residents, allowing them to do things like approve or deny zoning variances and to inform and review policy during meetings that are open to the public. Usually, members of local boards or commissions are solicited through open calls for volunteers, who submit cover letters and résumés outlining their expertise and why they are qualified to serve as a board member or commissioner. Occasionally they're just appointed because they know or have experience with someone on the appointing committee. Explore the boards and commissions that are active in your community; they're a great way to find local experts and to learn more about how the municipality's priorities and regulations are put into action. If your community doesn't have something like an urban forestry commission, you can always ask your city council to consider establishing one.

Showing Up Is Half the Battle

Chasing down your representative or municipal employees isn't the only way to get their attention. Your city government has a docket of public meetings and hearings at which you can voice your concerns or ask for more information. City councils, subcommittees, boards, and commissions hold regularly scheduled meetings to discuss and make decisions on a variety of local topics, and public meeting laws require that these sessions, their agendas, and their minutes are open to the public. Municipal departments also hold open forums to get input or answer questions on specific projects. These meetings are great opportunities for you and your group to attend and publicly show your support or concerns about an issue. For example, if your neighborhood coalition wants to preserve the trees in your community, keep an eye out for public notices announcing development plans. In most municipalities, there's a complex and opaque bureaucratic process that takes place whenever someone wants to build something. That something might be paving a new parking lot, putting up a new building, or making major renovations to an existing structure. A good number of mature trees get cut down because they're in the way of new development or because working around them would be complicated and expensive. When a developer or property owner proposes new construction or a building expansion, the city's planning department or zoning board often posts a notice on their website or sends letters to those living or working adjacent to the property, informing them of the project. These announcements include steps for stakeholders (that's you!) to ask questions and voice concerns to your community's zoning committee. Most cities have some form of a zoning board made up of elected or appointed individuals who review proposals, ask questions, impose restrictions on, and approve or deny new developments or major renovations. Part of their role is to consider the impact that proposed development has on the city as a whole and on abutting residents. Many times, those announcements go straight into the recycling bin (I'm guilty of that!), but these meetings provide a great opportunity for you to speak up and ask questions about the impact of the project, such as:

- Are any trees going to be cut down for this project?
- If so, why? Are there ways to avoid removing the tree(s)?
- If trees *must* be cut down, will trees be replanted nearby? If not, why not?

- If trees will be replanted, how many and how old will the new trees be? Can the developer plant more larger, more mature trees to help make up for the time it will take for new trees to contribute to the neighborhood?
- If the trees will not be replanted, how will the developer manage the increased presence of stormwater, heat, and poor air quality caused by the trees' removal?

Nearly all municipalities in the country have zoning codes, a set of rules for how people are allowed to use space. These rules cover everything from which areas can be used for parks versus factories to the minimum number of parking spots required for every unit of housing built. When changes are made to zoning codes or individuals request an exception to them, the zoning board will hold a hearing to discuss the proposed alteration. There is usually time allotted for public input, which is when you and your group can advocate for changes that will make your neighborhood more climate resilient. For example, a city zoning code might require that every one-bedroom unit must also come with a minimum of 1.5 parking spots. The average American pull-in parking spot is about 9 feet by 18 feet, or 162 square feet. For a building that has eight one-bedroom apartments, that's nearly 2,000 square feet of land set aside to store cars when they're not being used, and that number doesn't include the space required to enter, exit, or circle the parking lot. Parking minimums increase the cost of building new housing, capture land that could be used for greenspace, exacerbate the urban heat island effect, and increase flooding risks.

Cities of all sizes, from Buffalo and South Bend to San Francisco and Minneapolis, are getting rid of surface parking minimums, and it's about damn time! The next time your city's zoning codes are up for review, submit public comments asking for reduced parking minimums or join an existing organization—such as an affordable housing, climate, or safe streets advocacy group—and look for opportunities to amend the zoning code to dedicate less space to parked cars. Removing the minimum doesn't forbid new buildings from adding parking spots; rather, it just gives building developers more choice about how to use the space.

Removing parking minimums isn't the only answer for smart parking development. Other options include requiring developers to add shade structures or solar panels above parking spots, requiring the addition of cisterns—big tanks below the parking lot that hold on to stormwater runoff and slowly release it into the sewer system—and requiring greenscaping can reduce heat and flooding risks.

A heads-up: when you first start speaking up, the process can be demoralizing. Sometimes you'll be the only voice speaking on your position, or sometimes public officials might not take your assertion that change can happen seriously. But know that it's not you—it's the system. In most municipalities, public hearings for things like zoning variances or amending regulations can be seen as just a formality to satisfy a technical requirement; developers and committees are not always used to engaging with the concerns of stakeholders in meaningful ways. As new as it is for you to speak, it might also be new for them to listen. That's why it helps to pull in as many folks as you can to write in or show up and come equipped with the data and observations you've collected.

You won't always get the outcome you want through this process, and it helps to use your group's strengths to put pressure on this system from outside the bureaucratic process. Sometimes developers or contractors will agree to work around trees but then cut them down anyway because the consequence of doing so is less than the expense of following the rules or because there aren't specific rules requiring contractors or planners to check in with residents about cutting down trees. In Somerville, Massachusetts, contractors building out an urban cycle track for the Department of Transportation cut down thirty-seven mature sidewalk trees without informing residents or the city's community development division. These street trees were the only infrastructure providing shade for over a mile. Although the community was unable to save them, residents reached out to local media, their city councilors, and community groups that cared about neighborhood beautification and climate adaptation, and they held a well-attended memorial service for the trees. Responding to resident anger and a flood of local news stories, the mayor, city council, and relevant city departments responded to this show of frustration and disappointment by codifying a tree preservation ordinance that requires a permit before the felling of any noninvasive trees above a certain size. Tree preservation or protection ordinances are a way for your city to codify the importance of trees. Reach out to your city councilor and ask if there's one in the books. If there isn't, ask what it would take to get one to a vote before the city council.

Don't Ask, Don't Get

Don't assume that someone else has already raised the issue you're concerned about with the correct municipal division or that the city is actively working on it. Conversations, by email, phone, or in person, with the person or people in charge of the issue you're concerned about are the best way to figure out if the issue is on their radar. It's very possible that local government departments are already aware of the problem and are planning to fix it at some point, in which case your advocacy can hasten their follow-through. It's also possible that the issue is within their power to correct but they have no idea the problem exists. When my family moved into the block that we live on now, there wasn't a single sidewalk tree in sight. In fact, there was no evidence that tree boxes had ever been cut into the concrete. Chatting with neighbors who had lived on the block for decades, I learned that our street, on the very edge of the city, was often mistaken by officials as belonging to the adjacent municipality. Garbage pickup, snowplowing, and other municipal services have historically been inconsistent and often required resident advocacy to correct. Our block wasn't on the radar of the urban forestry division, and they hadn't known that they'd unintentionally excluded our block from the forestry master plan because they hadn't known our block was within their jurisdiction. After getting most of our neighbors on board with the idea of trees, I took photos of our gray and barren block and made our case to the city to be included in the next round of street tree plantings. Eight emails and six months later, we received four sidewalk saplings that are now thriving. Don't ask, don't get! Most of the time, things aren't going to be as easy or clear-cut as my neighborhood's tree example (although a surprising amount of time, if the project is small enough and you're able to find the right person, it really can be as easy as a few polite, persistent emails). In that case, you might need to do a little more digging to figure out if the local government is aware of or is already planning to address the issue—that's where calls to your municipality and councilor can be helpful.

The famous quote "You can't fight city hall" paints the bureaucracy of municipal government as so big and immovable that change isn't possible. But I think what that quote misses is that not every type of change needs to be framed as a "fight." Many do require a butting of heads and the application of legal and social resources, but for many municipal issues, lasting change can come from partnerships where both parties are able to agree on shared priorities. Your city councilor should be able to give you a sense of local government's priorities, and it's important to look for areas of overlap. For example, if elder health and wellness is a priority for your councilor or municipal departments, community cooling might be an overlapping priority. By cooling parks and public spaces, elders, who are more susceptible to the ill effects of heat, are more able to engage in community outside their homes, which contributes to their social well-being and overall improved health. If job training is a community priority, the municipality can support green infrastructure installations on public lands by hiring underemployed residents. Engaging groups who share your priorities—in the examples above, senior advocacy and workforce development programs, respectively—can strengthen both of your positions and increase your power by expanding your coalitions. The more the city sees you as a partner in generating information, ideas, and solutions, the more likely it is they'll pay attention to your concerns when you need them to.

In 2023, community advocacy groups West Street Recovery (WSR) and Northeast Active Collection (NAC) scored a major citywide victory when Houston's city council approved adding $20 million to the budget to address the city's long-standing drainage issues that worsened during recent periods of extreme precipitation. As Felix Kapoor of WSR and Alice Liu of NAC explain in their summary of the win, around 80 percent of Houston's "open drainage ditches are in communities of color, and for decades, these neighborhoods have dealt with frequent street flooding that turned into weeks of standing water, breeding mosquitoes, spreading pollutants, and impeding travel."[4] A big part of getting the city to acknowledge the problem of poor drainage through the budget was building and activating a broad coalition as a means of collecting information about impacts, inequity, and potential solutions. WSR and NAC trained residents on how to effectively participate in and present information at community meetings, and they leveraged flooding events as a means of drawing media attention. While the government of Houston agreed that drainage issues were a priority, it didn't dedicate enough resources to collectively planning regulations for at-risk communities, so residents and advocacy organizations built the plans themselves and used relationships with city councilors to get regulations designed and implemented.

Budget

To keep the community running and meet residents' needs, the city or town needs money raised through tax revenue, loans, and bond sales. Each year the mayor's office (strong mayor system) or the city manager's office (weak mayor system) puts together an annual budget for the city with input from each of the municipal agency heads.[5] The budget outlines how that tax revenue, and any debt the city has taken on through loans or bonds, will be spent and usually aligns with the administration's priorities. In most cases, it is the council that decides if the city will take on more debt, if the budget will pass as written, or if it will require adjustments to meet constituent concerns.

The budget process is important because it officially sets the local government's priorities for the next year and alerts government divisions to how much they have to spend on staff and projects. If you want to influence change, take the time to learn more about your city's budget process; you don't have to be a financial wizard, but you should seek to understand the resources available to the division responsible for addressing your areas of interest. If, for example, the urban forestry budget has been cut or level-funded, the likelihood that a robust urban forestry effort will be taken that year will be reduced. That's where it really helps to dig into your list of allies and see if anyone has expertise in budgets, local government, or finance. In my experience, every city structures its budget slightly differently, and it can be useful to have someone on board who can help you navigate the document.

There are two ways to intervene in the local budget. The first is in advance of the budget by working with your city councilor, other residents in your coalition, and municipal department employees to name your priorities and request that they're attached to a line in a specific department's budget. The municipal department heads can recommend that the requested line is added to the budget. The second is when the budget is released for review; at that time, you can request that the city council reject the budget unless amendments are made to fund your specific issue. In both cases, it's extremely unlikely that anyone is going to listen to you if you're working alone; rather, you'll need to show up with a large and noticeable coalition that represents a significant voting block or group with influence.

Municipalities will often host public meetings called "budget hearings" giving residents the opportunity to submit written testimony or speak. If only one or two individuals speak up for your issue, even if they represent a larger coalition, their message will get lost in the long list of other community priorities. But if person after person after person after person represents your request using similar language and talking points, you'll be more likely to grab the attention of decision makers. Volume matters.

Many municipalities now offer the option to participate in budget hearings via videoconferencing or with a digital hybrid option, which is great—I was recently able to attend and speak at a budget hearing for my city while doing dishes at home. Check out your municipal website for details or give the front desk of your municipality a call if you're not sure what the participation options are.

Participatory Budgeting

Increasingly, municipalities are rethinking who gets to decide how public dollars are spent and are moving toward a shared leadership and decision-making process called "participatory budgeting." First established in 1989 in Porto Alegre, Brazil, participatory budgeting is when the local government sets aside a quantity of money and then solicits project recommendations from residents. A committee combines like projects and removes unfeasible ones, such as those that would take place on private or state-held land. Residents then get to vote on which projects they'd like to see implemented.

The city of Nashville, Tennessee, launched participatory budgeting in 2023, and residents requested everything from the installation of sidewalks to improve walkability, to shade sails stretched out over a playground to protect children from the sun, to the placement of a giant xylophone in a park to spark joy and encourage public music.[6] Scrolling through the list of proposed projects, one would expect that residents would have wildly different visions for how their city ought to spend a few million, but more often than not, major themes emerge that otherwise would have gone unaddressed by the city.

Most participatory budgeting processes do not require that residents be registered voters to participate in the process. This policy allows unnaturalized immigrants, undocumented immigrants, and convicted felons to participate in local decision making in an unprecedented way.

Now that you have a bit more knowledge regarding how local government decisions are made and who makes them, you need to make a compelling case for why your issue requires city resources to implement, and you'll likely be working uphill. Some neighborhoods have a disproportionate influence on city officials than other neighborhoods; they may have community connectors who have a history of working with the city, a large number of donors to local politicians within their boundaries, or social or political power that comes from their health, wealth, or race. As a result, other neighborhoods without connectivity need to speak a bit more loudly to be heard. One way your coalition can gain traction on major issues is through pairing lived experience and expertise with the collection and interpretation of data.

CHAPTER 7

Collecting Data

IN AN IDEAL WORLD, your neighbors will sign on to support your cause, and your municipal and locally elected officials are ready and able to quickly respond to the climate mitigation and adaptation needs of your community. In reality, you will need to persuade people to act, and if you are trying to enact systems-level changes in your neighborhood, the key people to convince are your local government officials or institutions who have authority over infrastructure and resources.

Although convincing these decision makers is crucial, it can also be challenging to get them to pay attention to, prioritize, and act on your issue for many reasons. First, the decision maker, who is often a municipal employee working in a department such as public works or an elected official, might lack the knowledge to understand the complaint, especially if the issue crosses multiple types of expertise. Second, the town might not have the money or resources to investigate nonemergency issues, especially if said issues only seem to affect a handful of people or if the issues are brought up in the middle of the budget cycle. Third, the affected group may not be considered important by the decision makers. Maybe they tend not to vote or donate significantly to campaigns, are a minority of the population in terms of their opinions or needs, publicly oppose the elected or appointed officials in charge, or face systemic discrimination due to their religion, race, ethnicity, or class. Or maybe they're not on the municipality's radar at all. Fourth, the chain of responsibility for infrastructure improvements may be unclear to residents or to city employees themselves. For example, my city has a mobility division that oversees the sidewalks, an urban forestry division that handles the sidewalk trees, and a department of infrastructure and asset management that handles everything below ground except for the gas pipes, which are owned and managed by the local gas company. When dealing with an under-the-sidewalk gas leak that's killing street trees, it's not always immediately clear, even to city officials, who oversees what, who needs to be part of which conversations, or who should pick up the tab for repairs. Finally, sometimes inaction by the municipality or the institution is much cheaper than acting.

When my community pressured the gas company to fix its leaky infrastructure, at top of mind for all was that even the most basic repair to the half-mile stretch of 20-inch cast-iron pipe would cost more than $1 million. Gas infrastructure in my state is run by publicly traded companies that are estimated to lose about $8.9 million in leaked methane each year across the *entire* state.[1] Spending such a large amount to reduce a relatively small leak in a single community was not in the gas company's best interest. Doing nothing was much cheaper in two ways. First, it would save the company $1 million dollars. Second, making the repair would set a precedent that the company was open to fixing leaks that it was not legally obligated to fix.

There was a cost to inaction, though, even if the gas company was not the one to bear it. The leaks had killed a half-mile stretch of trees that would cost around $2,000 each to replace and maintain, and it would take several decades of care for those trees to reach maturity and give value back to the neighborhood. By the way, if you're feeling sticker shock at the price of trees, I feel you! Trees are expensive to plant, prune, and professionally maintain in the public right-of-way. A work crew is required to saw through the concrete and create a tree box, trees themselves can cost $150 to $350 depending on the "caliper size" (how big the trunk is), and then the tree has to be watered and monitored for three years until it is fully established. That said, the benefits in the form of cooling, air quality, and beautification are worth much more. Tree maintenance costs vary greatly across the United States, but it's still a significant expense, and as a result, many communities fail to fund it, putting their canopy at risk.

On top of destroying thousands of dollars of city infrastructure, the leaks contributed a steady stream of methane, a potent greenhouse gas, into the already warming atmosphere. While residents experienced the impacts of this infrastructure failure on a daily basis through hotter commutes and poor air quality, the impact was difficult to quantify and tangibly communicate to both the gas company and government officials. Exactly how many leaks were there, and where were they located? How many trees had been killed, and what would it cost to replace them? How much hotter was it on that side of the street compared to the side shaded by living trees?

Here's where data, in the form of maps, tables, charts, tallies, and testimonials, can close the gap between what you see as important and what those with decision-making authority think is important. Lawrence Hoffman, a geographic information system

(GIS) and data systems expert, often notes to me that "the power of data rests in who is holding it."[2] Being able to pair your lived experience and observations with maps and data gives you an edge in understanding both the challenges and the solutions needed and gives you the ability to identify and communicate your priorities.

In the dominant culture in the United States, data is understood in quantitative terms—as finite facts that inform universal truths. But even hard numbers that illustrate things that we can see and measure aren't always able to capture the impact on the human experience or tell the full story of how a place came to look as it does. Racist and classist beliefs held by historical decision makers led to our communities experiencing climate risk extremely differently today. Those same value systems have prioritized quantitative methods of understanding places, such as tabulating trees or number of cars, over other ways of understanding places, such as storytelling and community history. That's unfortunate, because community or traditional knowledge that originates with those most impacted by an issue can provide critical insights into challenges and potential solutions. Also, quantifiable data is vulnerable to manipulation and biased interpretation depending on how the data is gathered, who is gathering it, and ultimately how it is presented. Being able to connect numbers with stories that illustrate lived experiences is an important way of ensuring that your message offers an authentic, nuanced perspective.

Collecting and presenting data paired with lived experience can do a few things to move the needle toward change. First, data provides tangible supporting evidence of a community's lived experiences and the scope of an issue. By gathering data to show the widespread scale of the problem, community groups can build a case for why municipal officials should apply resources to address concerns. It also provides more information about the situation, which can help residents and decision makers determine the best solutions, such as improving storm drains, installing a cistern, planting green infrastructure, or removing pavement.

Second, data can highlight the disparities that exist within a city and prompt the necessary, but sometimes uncomfortable, dialogue that paves the way to justice. Across the country, cities and towns are signing up to participate in urban heat island mapping campaigns to better understand and visualize hyperlocal disparities. Traditional heat mapping uses satellite data that has a spatial resolution of 30 meters by 30 meters, which can obscure subtle differences between blocks or neighborhoods. During local Heat Watch campaigns, funded by the National Oceanic and Atmospheric Administration (NOAA) and designed and implemented by CAPA Strategies, volunteers collect air temperature data with sensors to produce street-by-street visualizations of how cities experience both heat and humidity. The data is compiled into publicly available maps and reports that visualize the urban heat island effect. Check out the NOAA website to view your community's street-by-street heat assessment; if your community isn't mapped, reach out to your municipal planning division and ask them to apply to become the next Heat Watch community via NOAA's website.[3]

When the Groundwork Richmond, Virginia, Green Team[4] was organizing around extreme heat, something they heard often from residents was, "Of course it's hot, it's always hot in Virginia!" But when youth presented residents with land surface temperature maps that showed how neighborhoods experience heat and asthma risk across the city, residents were deeply moved by the disparities they saw. Historically marginalized areas of Richmond, Virginia, were 16°F hotter than their wealthier, Whiter counterpart neighborhoods and had much higher instances of childhood and adult asthma. The heat itself didn't register as unusual with most residents, but the unfairness did, inspiring people to get involved in the upcoming Richmond master planning process to demand the city prioritize these hotter communities for infrastructure improvements over the next ten years.

Visualizing the disparities in who is exposed to flooding, poor air quality, increased fire risk, and extreme heat pushes people to ask, why? Why do things look the way they do? And why have conditions not yet changed? Groundwork's work through the Climate Safe Neighborhoods partnership suggests that even those who are skeptical of the existence of the climate crisis, institutional racism, or the need to address either can be deeply moved when faced with tangible proof of inequities in their own communities. Data that illustrates disparities can inspire people who usually aren't politically or environmentally active to join you in advocating for change by serving as a neutral platform for conversations about equity. Maps displaying local data can shift community challenges from a contentious "us versus them," "red versus blue," or "White versus Black" framing to a "there's a problem in *our* community, so what will we choose to do about it?" framing.[5]

Third, collecting data in the form of community oral histories and resident-selected images can add color and nuance to quantitative data, leading to more creative and culturally appropriate solutions. In 2018, the Acadiana Planning Commission in Lafayette, Louisiana, launched an intergenerational PhotoVoices project. PhotoVoices is an activity that engages the community in dialogue about local assets and opportunities. Using smartphones, digital cameras, or, in a pinch, disposable cameras, community members capture images around a site, question, or theme and pair those images with narratives about how they view the built environment. These stories and visualizations are then displayed and discussed during a community showcase event. The power of Pho-toVoices is threefold: it encourages participants to explore their surroundings from new perspectives, it builds a powerful platform for storytelling, and it establishes a visual, written, and oral record of the community that can be used to stimulate dialogue around a planning process.

The commission used the PhotoVoices process to identify community land use priorities along the Simcoe and University Avenue corridors, and although their primary goal was to find economic revitalization opportunities, residents brought rich perspectives on the potential for underutilized parcels of land to serve as key civic spaces. Something I love about using photos and oral history as a means of data collection is that it makes the process of evaluating assets and obstacles accessible to young children, who are often left out of neighborhood planning processes but who have valuable things to say about how they'd like to use public spaces. Children are regularly moved throughout a community by their caregivers with little agency, but due to their experiences, perspectives, and creativity, they have wonderful ideas about how to improve a space and a pretty big stake in decisions that will impact their futures, especially regarding the climate crisis.

Fourth, data can help you home in on a specific and concrete ask. In 2019, a group of Latina promotoras from the Globeville and Elyria-Swansea neighborhoods (GES) in Denver, Colorado, came together with Groundwork Denver to learn more about climate risk through maps.[6] The promotoras had long heard the complaints from neighbors about the lack of tree canopy cover: walks to the bus stop were hot, home cooling bills were high each summer, and the community lacked the beauty and curb appeal a closed canopy would offer. When the promotoras reviewed national land cover database maps of Denver County, they were the ones to point out huge disparities in tree canopy cover. The GES neighborhoods, which are majority Latino, had a tree canopy cover resting at around 1 percent. Across the river, in the aptly named Country Club neighborhood, the tree canopy exceeded 26 percent. Residents used this data to come up with a specific request to rally support from the community and bring to their city councilors and urban forestry division. Residents requested ten thousand trees planted within the borders of their neighborhood within the next ten years to bring their tree canopy cover up to 25 percent. Having a concrete ask as compared to a vague request such as "more trees" also gives you a benchmark by which to measure and evaluate your progress. When residents received an offer of one thousand trees from state forestry resources, they were able to quickly compare the offer to their ask and shift their advocacy approach to meet their goal.

Everyone's a "Data Person"

Not everyone thinks of themselves as a "data person," but as it turns out, data does not have to be a dense spreadsheet of numbers or a series of regressions. It's just a compilation of information that helps you understand why things are the way they are, and it's likely that you're already collecting and synthesizing data about your neighborhood all the time without even realizing it. When you choose to walk or bike down a shaded street instead of a sunlit one on a warm day, you're responding to data you've collected about which parts of your neighborhood feel hotter than others. After a rainstorm, you might preemptively cross the street to avoid getting your shoes wet because you know from experience that the crosswalk will be flooded out—that's data, too!

Valid and valuable data can be collected and analyzed by the average person. In this chapter, we talk about ways to quantify what you are seeing and experiencing in the built and natural environments to persuade decision makers. But quantitative data such as air temperature readings or number of storm drains becomes richer and more valuable when paired with qualitative data such as storytelling and community history. Comparing simple temperature readings across two neighborhoods allows you to answer the question of which neighborhood is hotter. Conversations with residents in each neighborhood help you identify which types of interventions will have a just and lasting impact in protecting the community from that heat. Both are data, both are within your capacity to collect and make sense of, and both are needed for fair and equitable adaptation to the climate crisis.

Community Science

Community science (also sometimes called citizen science) is the collection and analysis of data by members of the general public.[7] Often this work is done in conjunction with a trained scientist who provides support, interpretive assistance, and training on using tools and methods. There has been very reasonable pushback against the term *citizen science* in recent years because use of the term *citizen* linguistically excludes folks who are part of the community and eager to contribute to data collection efforts but who are undocumented or documented permanent residents.

Community science can be used to make tangible changes to local policies. For years, residents living adjacent to the Port of Elizabeth in Elizabeth, New Jersey, complained about the trucks traveling past their homes along the narrow, two-lane First Street in an attempt to avoid tolls on the highway. In 2014, residents and local community groups brought their concerns about rising asthma rates and pollution to scientists at Rutgers University's Center for Environmental Exposures and Diseases. "This community needs to know what's in our air. We want to know the truth. This area is big for asthma, maybe this is one of the things that's causing it," explained community activist and former truck driver Walter Leak. Robert Laumbach, director of the center's community outreach, trained resident volunteers in counting the number of trucks that passed along First Street as well as in using handheld air quality monitors to measure diesel particulate, exposure to which is linked to higher rates of asthma, cancer, birth defects, and cardiovascular issues.[8]

The data collected through community science was disturbing; as children walked to school, up to 120 diesel trucks per hour passed them by, coating the sidewalk in toxic gases and vapors from their exhaust pipes.[9] The coalition of residents, community groups, and Rutgers University representatives brought the data to the mayor and city council, who passed legislation banning large trucks from First Street and rerouting them to the highway. Colleges and universities, as well as certain environmental consulting firms, are often eager to work on interesting problems with community members. Reaching out to the planning, public health, and environment departments of your local university can sometimes connect you to scientists interested in conducting or supporting community science research in your neighborhood.

As you think about the questions that you would like to answer with data, keep the framing questions of "Who are my people?," "What is the change they need?," and "Why has this change not yet come about?" in mind. "Who are my people?" directs you toward those whose experiences you are trying to understand. "What is the change they need?" will help you understand what baseline data to look for. "Why has this change not yet come about?" will point you in the direction of who you need to present the data to. In the New Jersey example above, the "people" were those living or walking along the diesel truck route, the "change they needed" was to understand the source and severity of pollution and increased asthma rates in their community, and "change had not yet come about" because there wasn't yet compelling, tangible evidence of harm to inspire the city council and mayor to pass legislation re-routing the trucks away from First Street.

No- to Low-Tech Tools

Once you know the type of data you are going to collect, you will need to appraise the tools and methods by which you'll get access to needed information. Although I cover the technology you can use to do things like detecting gas leaks or measuring air quality a little later in this chapter, there are a number of free tools available to you for data collection.

Social Media

Social media is a surprisingly robust tool when you're getting started. Not only is it a great place to ask questions about the lived experience of residents in your community, but it can also act as a repository for information about community happenings. A friend of mine in New York who was concerned about flooding issues encouraged local residents to take photos of flooding in their neighborhood and tag it with a neighborhood-specific hashtag on Twitter (now known as X). It was a quick and easy way to create an organized database of powerful images to show how common the issue of flooding was after a rain event.

Oral History

Our communities look the way they do for a reason, and talking to longtime residents about changes to the community over time can help you understand the policies and people who have shaped the built environment. Asking simple questions about what the neighborhood or a specific street was like when a community elder was a child can give you valuable insight into the history of a place. Storytelling also has contemporary uses. Checking in with residents about things like their daily commutes, experiences with air quality, and how they handled a recent heat wave can clue you in to current needs you may not have identified through your own experiences.

Government Data

The US government is uniquely generous with the data it provides for free to the public. The American Community Survey pools together data on everything social and people-centered.[10] With a few clicks on the online portal, you can find data ranging from the owner occupancy rate of a neighborhood to the number of households with cars. By identifying factors such as income, transportation needs, and primary language spoken at home, you can better understand who your people are and how to connect with them. The US Department of Health and Human Services has a website that catalogs data on everything from heart disease to asthma rates, which can help you speak to decision makers about the health vulnerabilities in your community. The US Geological Survey (USGS) provides an absolute treasure trove of data about the built and natural environment. These types of data are valuable because they can help you paint a clear picture of who has access to what resources, such as lakes or parks, in your community. And all that is just the stuff that we can measure from here on Earth.

Right this minute, 438 miles above where you are sitting, there is an Earth observation satellite soaring through the thermosphere capturing data ranging from the temperature of your neighborhood sidewalks to how dense the tree canopy cover is across your city. Earth observation satellites, Landsats 8 and 9, which were launched by NASA, are zipping through space at 4.66 miles per second, making one complete orbit of Earth every ninety-nine minutes. The satellites are offset from each other, allowing them to make elegant loops around the planet and capture data on *every* square meter on Earth once every sixteen days. The data is then published online through the USGS National Land Cover Database.

You can go online and download all the data I mentioned above, right this very minute, for free! But all that free data, contained in Excel tables packed to the gills with digits, are useless to you unless they're translated into something easy to understand, such as a bar chart, graph, or map. You don't need to learn how to use geospatial mapping software like Esri ArcGIS or its open-source counterparts if you don't know it already. If you do want to learn, however, look into getting a GIS certification at a local community college or through an online course, or play around with open-source GIS tools such as QGIS. Luckily, there are plenty of others who do know how to use these tools and who are yearning to do it for a good cause. You just need to find them!

Getting Maps Made for You

Here's probably one of the biggest secrets in the book: getting publicly available data turned into maps can be incredibly expensive (think in the thousands of dollars per map) if you go through a private firm. But there's a free alternative many don't know about. One of the most amazing and untapped resources for data collection and analysis are the geography and urban planning departments of local colleges and universities. In both of these courses of studies, students at the undergraduate and master's levels are eager to hone their skills in real-world scenarios where they can be a help to others. Additionally, many of their degree programs require that students complete a "practicum" where they put their learning to the test by helping individuals, businesses, or local governments answer their geospatial questions. So, you can get the answers to your geospatial questions for free! Use a search engine to find a local geography, urban planning, urban studies, or geospatial science program in a city or university near you (example: "Urban planning department Missoula, Montana" or "Geography program, Colgate University"). The department staff websites will often have email addresses for those teaching courses about geography or GIS, but if they don't, it's totally okay to call the department's main line and ask. When you get the right email address, write to the professor to ask if they're open to having their students sharpen their skills by answering your geospatial questions via classwork or a practicum. When you reach out, give the person a bit of context about the challenge you are trying to address and the specific geospatial questions you're trying to answer, if you have them. "Where in town experiences the most severe heat in the summer?" and "Is air quality experienced similarly across racial and ethnic groups in our city?" are both strong geospatial questions.

If you don't have a specific question but have a general situation you want to learn more about, that is fine, too! Part of becoming a strong geospatial practitioner is helping others identify and answer their questions, so let the students practice by helping you tease out your questions. When you start work with the geospatial students, be sure to come in with the expectation that the process will probably be iterative. It is normal for completed maps and geospatial data to inspire additional questions that may need to be answered with additional data sets. Remember that data you personally collect is valuable and can be added to GIS maps as well. In Pawtucket and Central Falls, Rhode Island, students at the local school collected air temperature readings along major transportation routes. Groundwork USA's GIS specialist was able to add in the data points on a heat map of the city, allowing Groundwork Rhode Island to explore where along the route was most in need of cooling infrastructure.

Ready-Made Maps

A tremendous amount of data has already been collected, visualized, and put into online tools ready for your exploration. American Forest's online Tree Equity Score tool allows you to independently explore tree canopy cover in your city and see how many trees, by neighborhood, need to be planted to make the distribution of canopy equitable across the municipality. Heat Watch campaign volunteers collect data using ambient air sensor monitors at the same time and day over the summer. The data is compiled into publicly available maps and reports that illustrate how dozens of cities experience the urban heat island effect. The reports are online and publicly available to use.

Make Your Own Maps

Sometimes you can assemble key data just by taking a walk around your neighborhood with a pen and a paper map or notebook. For example, in areas where heat is a challenge, marking a hand-drawn map of your street with where trees and shade structures are installed can help you count how many pieces of cooling infrastructure exist and get a sense of the distance between them. This data becomes even stronger when you can compare data from a street of similar length and land use—commercial, residential, or industrial—in a different neighborhood. Even capturing images from online mapping platforms such as Google Earth can help you visualize differences in the built and natural environments. Figure

Figure 7-1: Google Earth image of a mixed-use neighborhood in northeast Portland, Oregon. On the right side of the image is a dense tree canopy cover, and on the left is a sparse tree canopy cover. (Map data: Google Earth © 2023 Landsat/Copernicus.)

7-1 is a screenshot from Google Earth showing a mixed-use neighborhood in Portland, Oregon. On the right side of the photo, even among the apartments, is a dense tree canopy cover; on the left side are fewer, smaller trees. The large parking lots on the left side of the photo will contribute to flooding and the urban heat island effect. The comparisons you can make with a simple map can be powerful tools because they force the often-uncomfortable question, "Why do things look different between these two places?"

You can also use this method to gather statistics about the presence or absence of various pieces of urban infrastructure, such as storm drains, streetlights, and stop signs. It can also be a valuable way of collecting information about resource distribution and condition. New Orleans, a city prone to flooding, has a startling lack of storm drains in and around the Seventh Ward. In some neighborhoods, you can walk for multiple blocks without seeing

Figure 7-2: This storm drain is both clogged and partially paved over. Images like this one can be powerful tools in communicating with the municipality and elected officials about ineffective infrastructure. (Photo by author.)

a single opportunity for water to enter the sewer. Those storm drains that do exist are often filled with trash or have their openings greatly narrowed by sloppily completed repaving projects (figure 7-2). Taking photos of damaged or inoperable infrastructure will enhance the data you collect, making the problem feel more tangible.

Tools that Cost Some Money

Some accessible tools are more specialized but still relatively affordable and simple to use. If heat is a concern, **infrared thermometers** (also called laser thermometers) are a quick and easy way to measure the temperature of an object at a specific point in time. They work by focusing infrared light through a lens and translating it into an electrical signal, giving you a numerical temperature reading—telling you how hot the surface of an object such as a sidewalk, grassy area, or car hood is. An infrared thermometer is a great way to understand what types and colors of materials retain and radiate heat. Similarly, an **air temperature sensor** can make sense of the myriad contributing factors—sun, wind, shade, humidity—that impact how humans experience the heat (think of how you feel if the temperature is 88°F with 20 percent humidity versus with 90 percent humidity). Both types of sensors run about $20 to $50 at time of writing and can be found online or at hardware stores.

Forward-looking infrared (also known as FLIR thermal) cameras clip to your phone or tablet and allow you to capture pictures of a location to visually compare the hotter (red, orange, and yellow) areas to the cooler (blue and purple) areas. A FLIR camera costs about $50 to $200 at time of writing. These cameras are useful for understanding which parts of your neighborhood are capturing and radiating heat and which areas have a cooling effect. The first time I used a FLIR camera, I was surprised to learn that grassy areas are not always that much cooler than parking lots. The hearty types of grasses we tend to plant for lawns are not efficient at cooling the surrounding environment when shorn short, especially compared to native grasses and yards planted with native wildflowers.

Another way to get a high-resolution understanding of heat in your community is by using **pocket weather sensors**. Ranging in size from an ice cube to a Pez dispenser, these sensors can be slipped into your pocket and take second-by-second measurements of everything from the ambient air temperature to humidity to the heat index (what temperature feels like to the human body). This data can be uploaded to your computer and then dumped into a simple online mapping software program such as Felt to visualize the temperature readings; areas that are hotter will appear as red dots, and cooler areas will appear as blue dots. This hyperlocal data can give you an extremely high-resolution picture of how heat is experienced in your neighborhood, from one footstep to the next.

Weather and government websites that show the air quality index (AQI) are useful tools for getting a neighborhood-wide picture of air quality conditions. But similar to the satellite heat data, the scale at which the AQI is usually reported can obscure important neighborhood-to-neighborhood variances in smoke or pollution. Lacking sufficient information about neighborhood-level conditions, some members of the US public have turned to nongovernmental air quality monitoring networks, such as PurpleAir, to assess their exposure to particulate matter, toxins, and smoke in the air.[11] PurpleAir collects data from indoor and outdoor **air quality sensors** placed on specific buildings within a neighborhood, including those owned by customers, and publishes real-time mobile and web maps with the results.

Finding Resources

The most valuable resource you have is the people who are invested in this problem. They might be members of your household, your friends, your neighbors, or people with whom you were put in touch through community connectors. These people are going to have a wealth and diversity of knowledge, and you will end up with a wiser plan to get that data with their help.

When the gas company denied that any leaks existed in my neighborhood, my community coalition knew the only option was for us to test for gas leaks ourselves. The cost of a portable sniffer, a tool that allows you to measure the percentage of methane in an area, was outside what anyone in our group could afford (though there are now some simple models available for purchase online for as little as $40), and even if we had one, we didn't know how to use it or communicate the results. Luckily, Randi, our neighborhood's community connector, was able to call an acquaintance, Bob, who worked for a gas repair advocacy group. Bob's organization was hired, often by municipalities, as a third-party gas leaks tester to identify and prioritize pipeline repair. He was willing to bring his gas sniffer along on the condition that we learned how to collect and communicate about the data ourselves.

On a rainy Friday morning, Bob took Randi and me out with his portable gas detector and taught us how to identify and measure the amount of methane in each one of the empty tree wells (figure 7-3) and along cracks in the sidewalk. Natural gas is distributed through a series of large pipes—between 20 and 50 inches in diameter—laid end to end and buried beneath the street or sidewalk. Smaller pipes branch off from that main transmission line, bringing the gas into your home. While there should be no methane present in tree boxes or anywhere outside of the pipes, within three hours we had measurements showing the presence of methane near every pipe joint along the half-mile stretch, most in the tree-strangling range and none in the explosion-risk range. The data suggested that the pipe had many small leaks to be fixed. Thanks to the resource that is Bob, we gained the ability to explain to other members of our coalition where the pipe was located, how to identify where the underground joints of the pipe likely were, how to tell if the pipe had recently been serviced or repaired, and where methane is likely to get trapped underground when a leak is present.

Figure 7-3: Randi uses a portable gas sniffer to measure methane leaks. (Photo by author.)

What to Do with that Data

Once your data is collected, it is time to share it with others. Start by sharing it with those who worked with you to gather the information. It is important that people see the results of their efforts—doing so keeps up morale, builds a sense of pride, and makes people feel valued for their contributions. Then, discuss the data with the other allies and stakeholders to begin the process of building out a vision. That can be through a community event such as a block party, a digital or paper newsletter, or a more formal presentation. Some questions you might consider discussing when reviewing the data with stakeholders are:

- What does the data tell us about our question or challenge?
- Is there anything surprising about what we are seeing?
- Ideally, what would be different about what we are seeing?
- Who has the ability to authorize or facilitate the change we need?
- How will we know if we've been successful in facilitating the change we need? (For example, will the pavement be gone, a park developed, trees planted?)
- Who else needs to see this data, and what context do they need to fully understand what it means to the community?

The answers to these questions will help you and your community develop a specific ask, which you'll need to clearly articulate the ways in which people with decision-making authority, such as municipal departments and elected officials, can meet your needs. When presenting the data to allies, stakeholders, city officials, elected officials, or other decision makers, take the time to explain what the source of the data is, including the date it was collected, how it was collected, and what you believe the data to mean. From there, you have a shared platform for conversations about change.

From Data to Solutions

In negotiation and dispute resolution teachings, there's a common metaphor about pie. If you're trying to split up a pie among several people, unless individuals get equal amounts of pie, some will get more and some will get less. But, if the parties work together, they might be able to secure a larger pie to divide, benefiting all. When working with a coalition of stakeholders to make data-informed decisions, you might run into situations where everyone comes to consensus about the meaning of the data, but they view the available resources for solutions as fixed and in conflict with one another. If I get a big slice of pie, you get a smaller one. If we plant trees in my neighborhood, your neighborhood won't get any because the urban forestry budget is fixed. But, as much as possible, I encourage you to look for opportunities to "enlarge the pie" as you transform your data into potential solutions. The information you have and the solutions you develop should be in constant conversation.

In the tree example, the resources can appear pretty fixed. If the urban forestry division has a certain budget, more trees planted in one neighborhood will mean fewer trees planted in a different neighborhood during that season. Trees are expensive; it costs around $1,500 to $2,000 per tree to get one planted and established, and that isn't inclusive of other costs, like cutting the sidewalk boxes in the concrete or special visits from arborists if the tree falls ill. Cities such as Indianapolis, Indiana, are launching programs to help enlarge the pie of resources to get more sidewalk trees in the ground by engaging residents in the care and maintenance of those trees. Their community forestry program allows residents to "adopt" twenty or more trees in a neighborhood. The city pays for the planting and overall maintenance, but in exchange residents do door-to-door outreach to get neighbors on board with the plantings, water trees planted on private property, and agree to call in dead or sick trees so that they can be cared for by a city contractor. The fixed resources (or the "pie") were expanded by thinking creatively about how to distribute the work around this climate adaptation intervention.

Additionally, you might consider enlarging the pie in regard to the types of problems your solution can solve. My gas leak coalition brought together a large stakeholder group to review the data Randi, Bob, and I had collected during a site visit to the street. Our group included a city councilor from the infrastructure committee, Mothers Out Front members, urban forestry committee members, a city engineer, gas company representatives, and the executive director of a climate mitigation nonprofit focused on gas line emissions. At first, our stakeholder group thought a pipeline replacement was what was needed because the data we collected showed that the gas leaks were plentiful and wide reaching. The city estimated that the cast-iron pipe was approaching its eightieth birthday and was prone to a Whac-A-Mole style series of leaks over time as the jute linking the pipe joints deteriorated from age—when one leak was patched, another would likely spring up. Ultimately, members of our group who were focused on climate mitigation wanted to push the city to stop using natural gas altogether over the next five to ten years. In that case, it did not make sense to demand millions of municipal and private-sector dollars be spent installing a new piece of durable infrastructure if we simultaneously were looking to decommission existing gas infrastructure. Doing so would leave less money for the transition to electrical infrastructure. Instead, the group settled on a relatively inexpensive ask that met all our needs: a thin, plastic sleeve run through the interior of the pipe to stem current and future leaks. This solution, which would not require excavation to reach the pipe, would also limit disruption to commuters, people who live next to the leaks, and the city. The city could confidently replant the trees, knowing their investment was safe from underground harm; the gas company would save money by avoiding a costly excavation; and the methane emissions would be greatly reduced. We enlarged the pie to benefit multiple types of stakeholders by moving away from a single fixed solution (replacing the pipe) that would mostly benefit the trees to a more creative solution that took advantage of technology to meet multiple needs at once.

When using data to come up with possible solutions, be sure to involve the full suite of stakeholders, including your experts, allies, and naysayers. Multiple perspectives are key to coming up with fair, wise, and lasting solutions. While many solutions will be discreet, like the gas leak example above, we can't forget about the role of policy in this work. Many of the harms we're looking to solve are the result of intentional policy decisions that were made decades—or even centuries!—ago. Like data, policy might seem complicated, but also like data, it's just a collection of ideas about implementing community values.

CHAPTER 8

Systems Change

The data you collect is key to intervening in the way deci-sions are made and resources distributed at the local level. Gener-ally, before they commit to spending tax dollars on a new program or policy, local government agencies want to understand both the scope and scale of the problem, as well as how they will identify and measure the success of an intervention. If a neighborhood has few trees, the urban forestry division might evaluate the number of spots suitable for new trees before it commits to planting. Once planted, the number of surviving saplings might be measured five years later by the department as a means of assessing success. Before installing protected bike lanes, the transportation division might evaluate the number of cyclists and motorists on the road over a twelve-month period and then take the same measurements after the protected lanes are built to see if improved bike infrastructure has impacted the way people get around. But municipalities don't always consider all relevant data and information before launching an intervention, and that can have disastrous consequences either for the people living there or the intervention itself.

When I finished college, I packed my things and moved back to New York City. The first room I rented was in a fifth-floor walk-up building in West Harlem. The apartment was advertised as having a "river view" because if you pressed your face up against the window bars and strained your eyes to the left, you could see the faintest glint of the Hudson River shimmering between the other buildings. The neighborhood, mostly Dominican, was hot—the nearest open space was the massive blacktop playground of the local elementary school, and the community lacked street trees that would have provided the consistent shade found in wealthier neighborhoods at either end of the train line.

That fall marked the second year of Mayor Michael Bloomberg's Million Trees NYC Campaign, a massive urban forestry project to plant one million trees across the city's five boroughs in ten years. Our long, shadeless block fit the bill for improvement: wide sidewalks, no low-hanging power lines, and in a community vulnerable to and suffering from extreme heat and poor air quality. Early one morning, I left my apartment for work, and by the time I returned home there were saplings planted every 15 feet or so from Broadway to Amsterdam Avenue. It was surprising how quickly the cement had been cut, soil hauled, and trees planted. In the year that I'd lived in the neighborhood, I had never seen a flyer, door tag, or representative from the New York City Planning Department alerting the community to the coming change. The next morning, I galloped down the stairs, pushed open the heavy metal door, and found that the crown of each newly planted tree had been snapped off and hurled into the street. When I asked what happened, our first-floor neighbor, a freckled octogenarian who could reliably be found perched in her window, simply shrugged and replied, "They didn't ask us."

The trees on my block weren't the only ones to experience a

destructive response. Across New York City, residents who were frustrated with changes made to their neighborhood without their input or consent snapped, uprooted, and cut down newly planted saplings, baffling city officials who believed they were doing the right thing by siting trees. The data clearly showed that these places needed improved canopy cover if residents were to have the cooling, air-clearing infrastructure of wealthier neighborhoods. This was justice driven by data. And that was exactly the problem.

Data is important; love it or leave it, it's the language that decision makers speak in and is a key part of effecting lasting, measurable change. But leaning so far into the data that you neglect to center those who would be most impacted by your ideas perpetuates harms to groups already awash in environmental burdens. Successful and just interventions require solutions designed and driven by the people directly impacted by climate risks. Sometimes those people are going to be you and members of your coalition, but sometimes they'll be others whose wants and needs have long been ignored and need to be considered. As cities develop their climate resilience plans, it's critical for you to be involved in shaping the policies and solutions for your community and to use the resources you have to support and make room for those often left out of policy making.

Policies are courses of action that your municipality has chosen to adopt through guidelines, regulations, funding priorities, or laws. Everything in your neighborhood—from where the parking lots are located, to how tall the buildings are, to which neighborhoods have street trees—stems from an intentional decision guided by policies. Sometimes decisions were made a century ago and sometimes they were codified last week, but in all cases, those decisions can be changed to reflect current or aspirational values and norms. At their core, policies are just ideas the government has decided will help them achieve certain goals. And you know who has good ideas about how to change things for the better in your community? You. Through your collection of data, your understanding of local history, and your conversations with community members, you're well suited to take the information you've gathered and transform it into municipal policy ideas.

Policy comes about via your elected and municipal officials, and there are lots of opportunities for you and your coalition to intervene in decisions that are being made. Understanding how policy making happens will help you understand how to intervene. When you begin this work, it's helpful to focus on four major areas for intervention: master plans, greening or resilience plans, local ordinances, and zoning. These four areas of intervention are how the bulk of decisions are made about how community needs are prioritized and resources distributed.

Master plans (also known as comprehensive plans) are long-term policy documents orchestrated by your planning department to outline your municipality's priorities, goals, and strategies over ten, fifteen, or twenty years. Divisions within the local government, such as transportation and public works, use the master plan to guide their work across the city and to request the funding they need, but they aren't legally bound to enact what's in the plan because the plan is not legislation. The municipality writes the plan, publishes a draft for public review, and then holds a comment period (sometimes written only, sometimes a combination of written and a public hearing) where residents can recommend modifications for consideration.

Greening/resilience plans are relatively new to the scene. While master plans might address sustainability goals or have resilience sections, increasingly, cities are creating separate plans to focus on resilience, carbon emission reductions, and climate adaptation policies. They often have recommendations about changes to zoning codes, adoption of resilience-focused ordinances, and establishment of programs related to sustainability or climate adaptation. Greening plans are, at time of writing, rarely funded and are meant to be in conversation with the goals set forth in the municipality's master plan. When plans are funded, the money usually comes from the municipal budget. Similar to master plans, resilience plans often have public comment periods or community outreach requirements, which are great opportunities to get involved.

Local ordinances are laws passed by your city or town council and cover everything from property taxes to parking requirements. There are two ways to intervene in local ordinances. The first is to work with your councilor to draft new ordinances that cover the issues you're concerned about. The second is to keep abreast of the ordinances going before your council and work with your councilor to recommend changes or amendments before an ordinance goes to a vote. This latter way is sometimes tricky because consideration for the draft may not explicitly be called out in the council meeting agenda.

Zoning refers to ordinances, regulations, and plans that dictate how land—either specific properties or larger areas of the community—can be used. Land can be zoned for commercial, industrial, or residential uses, and some zoning laws can regulate development details, such as requiring that new housing construction come with a certain number of parking spots or that a certain number of square feet be dedicated to stormwater capture. Zoning laws are designed and passed by your city council or zoning board (sometimes referred to as a land use committee). Not all municipalities (looking at you, Houston, Texas!) have zoning; in those communities, land use decisions are often covered by local ordinances instead. Master plans and ordinances are fairly straightforward, but zoning is usually approached through a combination of committees, plans, and ordinances. For example, the planning division may produce maps and plans for land use that the city council must approve, while residents or businesses seeking variances to the approved plans might need to petition a zoning board composed of residents, councilors, or both.

Master plans, greening plans, ordinances, and zoning infrastructure are the most common mechanisms through which you can change the way decisions are made and resources distributed at the local level. That list isn't exhaustive, though, so you should be on the lookout for other opportunities to get involved. For example, in 2020, Denver voters passed ballot measure 2A to fund climate resilience programs. The 0.25 percent tax increase raises an estimated $40 million dollars per year, and decisions are made about how that funding is distributed, in part, via a resident advisory board. If you have the time and the interest, look for opportunities to join decision-making boards and committees within your community.

Example Asks and Ordinances

All that said, events such as votes on climate ballot measures don't happen every day, so for your average community, it makes sense to realize your priorities through existing municipal infrastructure. Below are a few examples of "asks" that you and your coalition members may consider advocating for and the processes or people you'd need to influence to make those asks happen. This list isn't exhaustive; rather, it is meant to help you connect your ask to the policy-making mechanism that will help you realize your goal. In the endnotes, I've included links to relevant ordinances and policy documents because it's helpful to have examples from other communities to present to decision makers. Concrete examples prove that change is possible and is already being adopted by other communities (so what are *we* waiting for?), something that can be a motivating factor for elected or government officials who are worried about the feasibility of new programs, policies, and ordinances. Also, it's easier to modify existing policies and ordinances than it is to draft them from scratch. Remember that for each intervention you introduce, consider the five types of capital as a way of identifying which other stakeholders need to be at the table when your ask is being developed and considered.

The Ask: New Local Ordinances that Improve Biking and Walking Infrastructure

The What: Petition your city or town council to draft, introduce, and pass ordinances that ensure that transportation improvements address pedestrian and cyclist needs along with those of cars. Most municipalities have a regular schedule for road and sidewalk repairs, and some cities have ordinances that link improvements to cycling and pedestrian infrastructure, such as quick-build bike lanes or curb cuts, to road repaving.

The Why: The hotter it is, the less likely people are to walk, cycle, and take public transportation and the more likely they are to drive. Cars, however, generate a substantial amount of waste heat via their combustion engines, making walking along roads or active parking lots hotter than areas without running cars.[1] The more heat there is, the more cars there are; the more cars there are, the more heat there is. Ordinances that allocate resources toward cycling and walking infrastructure help reduce the number of cars on the road, thus reducing the urban heat island effect and improving air quality.

Example Ordinance: In 2019, the city council of Cambridge, Massachusetts, passed the nation's first "Cycling Safety Ordinance," which requires the city to add permanent, protected bike lanes to major streets during scheduled reconstruction.[2] The ordinance is expected to result in 25 miles of new, protected bike lanes over seven years.

The Ask: Modify the Parks Master Plan to Include Splash Pads and Misters When Parks Are Built or Redeveloped or to Replace Aging Pools

The What: Departments of parks and recreation often produce master plans for large individual parks (think Prospect Park in Brooklyn, New York, or Golden Gate Park in San Francisco, California) or the entire parks system. These plans cover everything from the presence (or absence!) of drinking fountains to the repair, replacement, or decommissioning of park infrastructure. If your community is vulnerable to heat, work with your coalition to submit recommendations that the parks department modify its master plan to prioritize the installation of splash pads and misters at local parks and playgrounds when they are built or renovated and the transition of decommissioned or failing pools into splash pads instead of leaving them shuttered.

The Why: Diving into a pool on a hot summer's day can be a great way to beat the heat, but there are a few challenges to using pools as a climate adaptation strategy that might have you looking toward misters. Increasingly, municipalities are decommissioning pools that have reached the end of their lives as pools are expensive to rebuild or maintain. Even if your local pool stays open, that doesn't mean it's usable by those most in need of relief. Some residents at risk of heat-related illnesses are unable to swim or have disabilities that keep them from getting to or enjoying the pool. People who work outside the home may not be able to get to the pool during the hours it is open, and nationwide lifeguard shortages are reducing those open hours significantly. Splash pads and misters are great alternatives to pools. They provide accessible, intergenerational access to cooling down; don't require skilled personnel, such as lifeguards, to oversee them; can be run day or night; and, compared to pools, are relatively cheap to install and maintain. Splash pads require a fair amount of drainage to prevent stagnant water or localized flooding, but misters—which express a fine water vapor similar to what you might see sprayed over vegetables in the grocery store—require little to no drainage while offering similar benefits to splash pads.

Example Ordinance: The Park Improvement Projects Master Plan developed by the Louisville, Kentucky, Parks and Recreation Department calls for the installation of "spraygrounds" (interactive splash pads and misters) in the redevelopment and construction of parks. Although not binding, the master plan does guide the investment in the Louisville park system, which currently enjoys more than thirty spraygrounds.[3]

The Ask: Modify the Department of Transportation's Policies and Guidelines to Include Nature-Based Stormwater Retention

The What: Working with your city or town councilor and your coalition, interface with your local department of public transportation to influence policies and roadway design guidelines to include landscaped medians.

The Why: Replacing barren soil in medians with drought-tolerant wildflower mixes, trees, or low-maintenance shrubs increases stormwater retention and reduces heat. Your local department of transportation (DOT) is most likely responsible for roadway medians, although some may be under the control of the state DOT. Even though the DOT updates its policies and guidelines on varying schedules, these don't *always* go out to the public for comment in the way a municipality's master plan might. So, to open the conversation about design guidelines and policy changes, you and your coalition will have to build a relationship with someone in the department. If the city or town council—which, as a reminder, approves the department's budget—is on board with the changes, the department is more likely to give the demands more serious consideration.

Example Ordinance: The City of Chicago's Department of Transportation has adopted landscaped medians as part of DOT infrastructure policies and guidelines.[4] Now, as a way of contributing to the department and the city's climate adaptation goals, when roadways are rebuilt or redesigned, the city installs trees or plants in the median, depending on safety considerations. The recently completed 130th Street and Torrence Avenue rebuild includes trees, shrubs, and plants to calm traffic, capture vehicle exhaust particulate, retain stormwater, and reduce the urban heat island effect.

The Ask: Modify the Zoning Ordinances to Require that "Cool Roofs" Be Installed on New or Majorly Renovated Buildings

The What: Adopted everywhere from Denver, Colorado, to Houston, Texas, cool roof policies require that newly built or existing buildings use reflective roofing materials or paint to bounce away the sun's rays. Requiring buildings to adopt cool roof technologies can be accomplished through ordinances that modify the city's building or zoning codes. This is another example of where you and your coalition will want to work closely with your city or town council to make the case for adopting the ordinance and provide examples of success in other communities.

The Why: According to the US Environmental Protection Agency, properly applied white roof materials can reflect up to

75 percent of the sun's energy compared to just 5 percent for a standard black asphalt roof.[5] Reflecting the sun's radiation both reduces the air temperature around buildings and reduces cooling costs for those inside, ultimately lowering carbon emissions and energy burdens.

Example Ordinance: In 2015, the Houston, Texas, city council modified its building code to require that cool roofs be installed on new or renovated commercial buildings.[6]

This short list is meant to give you a few examples of how to place your ask within specific municipal policy systems. But remember that the changes you seek, just like the Million Trees NYC campaign, might not be greeted warmly if those who are most impacted aren't involved in making changes to policies and programs. In the climate adaptation, greening, and nature-based solutions world, one of the biggest unintended consequences to changing the built environment through green infrastructure is called green gentrification.

Displacement

"Green gentrification" is the notion that as environmental conditions improve via the addition of green infrastructure, such as parks and trees, rent will rise and low- to moderate-income people will be displaced from their homes. Gentrification and displacement necessarily occur in places where housing prices have long been artificially depressed by municipal, state, and federal policies. Low-income people and people of color have been routinely forced, through restrictive zoning, redlining, municipal laws, and restrictive covenants, to settle in places that were already less desirable because of their proximity to industrial pollution, vulnerability to flooding, or lack of greenspaces. Those places have long had both greater environmental justice threats and rents and housing prices to match.

In recent years, studies have shown that greenway parks like New York City's High Line, the Atlanta BeltLine, and Houston's Buffalo Bayou Park contribute to rising rents and displacement in the neighborhoods where they're located.[7] Cities with urban forestry programs often quantify the value of trees by noting how they contribute to increased property values. That's great news if you're looking to sell or get equity out of your home; it's not so great news if you're trying to buy, are paying increasing property taxes, or are dreading an annual rent increase from your landlord. When your home is on the line, how much is that new tree really worth to you?

Generally, I dislike the term "green gentrification" because it places accountability on the trees and rain gardens instead of the residential and commercial landowners who unjustly profit from public investments in infrastructure by choosing to raise rents. It's not the trees causing the rents to rise; it's the landlords. It's not the improved desirability of a place that's the problem (ideally, shouldn't we all get to live somewhere nice?); it's the destruction of communities resulting from increased housing prices.

No climate resilience strategy, policy, or intervention is fair and just unless it centers community priorities and includes provisions to address potential consequences such as displacement. If greening is a priority in your community but would put you or your neighbors at risk of displacement pressures, it is vital to partner with housing advocacy groups to screen for unintended consequences of your desired intervention and to find ways to further both housing stability and climate adaptation. Louisville, Kentucky, which is known for predatory renting and unfair housing practices, has recently passed renter protections for families.[8] Resident housing advocates in historic Black neighborhoods in Louisville are pushing for additional policies to stem displacement. The Historically Black Neighborhood Ordinance would create a process by which to determine if development in historically Black neighborhoods in Louisville would likely lead to displacement; if so, the developer will be denied access to municipal property, financial support, and resources.[9] Strong protections for renters and low- to moderate-income homeowners make up the foundation of just and wise changes to climate adaptation. If your community isn't at risk of displacement but you're advocating for resilience policies at the municipal level, partner with housing advocacy groups as a means of preventing unintentional harm to other communities.

No one has the complete and undeniable approach to greening our cities without unintended consequences, but there are ways to be thoughtful about your impact and use your collective power to advocate for resilience policies and programs that benefit all. As cities and states develop their climate resilience plans, they must have residents and local advocates at the table and include multipronged strategies that allow for wealth building for those long kept out of the housing market due to their race or class, the stabilization of rents, and a push toward establishing more decommodified housing through the support of community land trusts and housing cooperatives. They must allow for the creation of local jobs without disproportionately siting toxic industry in Black, Brown, immigrant, and low-income neighborhoods. They must provide for transportation and commerce without exposing those most vulnerable to plumes of black carbon-laden exhaust. Just and effective solutions both meet the demands of the climate crisis and do so without causing harm to those who have already weathered the burden of injustice for too long. If a neighborhood's flood risk is reduced but long-term residents can no longer live there, one crisis has just been swapped out for another.

Just as it can be difficult to know how to effectively intervene in the climate crisis, it can be just as hard to know where you can step in to further fair and just solutions that avoid causing harm to others. What you can do is flex your privilege by naming the people, interests, and organizations that are missing from the room when climate solutions, policies, or local funding distribution is discussed and then working to make space for them in those rooms. The term *privilege* (as in "check your privilege") has become a means of admonishing others for the resources and access they have due to elements somewhat outside of their control. Your race, ethnicity, color, gender identity, sexuality, English language proficiency, size, income of origin, educational attainment, ability, and place of birth all award you a complex combination of privileges that can be utilized to advocate for yourself and on behalf of others. I see privilege as, yes, something to be aware of, but also as a call to action to use what you have to make space for those who don't have the resources, social capital, or access to power that you do. And the hope is that others who have what *you* do not possess will make space for you, too.

Using your privilege for the good of others starts by noticing what resources you have that enable you to fully participate in civic life and giving some thought as to what might happen if you didn't have those resources. For example, if you attend community meetings held by your city about siting a park, you might notice that only English is spoken by the presenters even though there might be a large Spanish-speaking population where you live. Your privilege is English proficiency, and if you didn't have it, you might not have an opportunity to express your opinions to the municipality or sway their decision making. You can then use your English proficiency to reach out to the meeting hosts and request that the meetings be made accessible to Spanish speakers.

As you continue along your journey in fighting against the climate crisis, use whatever resources or privileges you have not just to further change, but also to make sure those who will be most impacted by that change are actively in the room and are being listened to. Drawing attention to the lived experience and ideas of those often excluded from processes is a huge and undervalued step toward operationalizing the values of equity and justice.

Conclusion: In It for the Long Haul

As we finish our time together in this book, it's important that I leave you with a sense of your own power to change things without shying away from the truth that, when it comes to the climate crisis, we're up against a lot. One of the hardest things to accept in this work is that you're never going to see the end of it. Stewarding the earth, mitigating our damage to the planet, adapting to a changing climate—it's all the labor of generations. It's taken nearly two hundred years and billions of dollars of investment in antidecarbonization lobbying to get us to this point, so it's going to take a long while to figure out how to adapt to our ever-changing reality. And this adaptation doesn't happen in a vacuum. It is further complicated by the sexism, racism, classism, and ableism that increase the vulnerability of some over others. With hard truths like that, it's normal to worry, to feel grief or rage, and to have moments of hopelessness, even when you're out there successfully battling heat, flood, and fire.

So, what do we do? We can't realistically shy away from these feelings, but simultaneously, we can't bring change about while lingering in them. Like any large and daunting journey, climate action has the potential to tire you and to burn you out if you don't build the skills and habits required to keep your flame alight. As intentional as you are about understanding history, collecting data, and building your coalition, you need to be just as intentional in finding joy and direction in the work so that you can stay invested for the long haul. Luckily, a few simple, concrete practices—communication, rest, and celebration—can be integrated into your climate work to keep your and your coalitions' energy and momentum going.

Communication

If you've ever sat in a poorly run meeting, class, or training, you may have left feeling unsure about why you were there and what you were supposed to do. That feeling is *exhausting* and a recipe for burnout. Clarity about the group's shared goal and the skills and actions needed to accomplish it (even if that action is decision making) helps members of your coalition avoid the mental and emotional fatigue that comes with trying to figure out if they should be doing something or not. If your coalition is burning energy trying to figure out if they're supposed to be acting or if the thing they're doing is actually helpful, they won't have the energy to actually do what needs to be done to effect change. Similarly, without a clearly defined purpose, it can feel like you're spinning your wheels and failing to make progress, which is extremely discouraging.

During your meetings or events, take time to restate the vision of how things will be different after your intervention and make sure that everyone is still on board. If people don't know or agree with what the group is trying to accomplish and how they can contribute to the goal, they aren't going to stick around. Similarly, make sure that it's clear to participants how their participation in certain tasks moves everyone closer to the stated vision. For example, if the action is to get city council members to sign onto an open letter to the Urban Forestry Division, how does that further the group's vision of a cooler neighborhood? If an action doesn't connect to the goal or the vision, reconsider if it should be done at all.

Be Organized and Consistent in Your Communication

Part of keeping people engaged in this work is making sure you keep everyone updated, even through the inevitable lulls in a project or campaign. One of the easiest ways to keep momentum is to set up a consistent meeting schedule (same time and day) in person or via videoconferencing. When you pull your group together, the same good meeting practices that you might use at school or work apply to coalition meetings. For each get-together, be sure to define the purpose of the meeting, set an agenda, and take turns doing housekeeping tasks (such as note taking, time keeping, or hosting). Also be sure to close the meeting by restating any decisions that were made and action items that were identified.

Follow up with an email summary so that members of the coalition can keep up with what has happened, get a sense of what's next, and know how to jump back in, even if they've taken a break. Communicating clearly and economically about what the group knows, what's next, and what is needed by when is a way of leaving the door open to those who may need to come in and out of this work. People get sick, lose or start new jobs, or have other obligations they must tend to that might cause them to temporarily step back from the coalition. Their absence (or yours!) shouldn't be viewed as a lack of commitment to this work, but instead recognized as part of being a human with competing priorities. Knowing that they can take a break and then easily reintegrate into the work is a way to keep others (and yourself) committed through the twists and turns that life throws at us all.

Share Success Stories

Real, positive, powerful change is happening across the United States this very minute! Even though successes are racking up from coast to coast, the enormity of how much further there is to go can be discouraging. Sharing news stories about successful climate policies, programs, and interventions can both reignite the belief that change is possible and give you, your friends, and members of your coalition new ideas for local solutions. Use your meetings, email listserv, or social media groups to share local and national stories of progress. When you've successfully made a change, big or small, share that, too! Everything—from that rain barrel you installed on the side of your building to the tree you planted—serves as an important and motivating sign of progress to others. Make sure to take before and after pictures to send out or even invite others over to see the results of your project in person.

Rest

The world is literally and figuratively on fire, so it's reasonable if you feel the need to do everything, everywhere, all at once. But pace yourself. You're not going to have the impact that you desire if you burn out and stop doing the work altogether. Stepping back from a project or choosing to not get involved with a new one isn't a sign of failure; rather, it can be a helpful boundary that preserves your energy for future action. Also, remember that whether it's composting or getting city council members to make good on their funding promises, most climate interventions require some type of maintenance, and you need to include that in your energy expenditure budget. If you can only commit to doing one thing from this book because you don't have the energy to do more, that's fine! That's one thing that wasn't being done before. If you need to rest and step away from the work entirely, do that and come back later at a scale and energy level that works for you in that moment.

Lean on Your Community

If this work feels too big to engage in, remember that you don't have to and shouldn't do this work alone. One way to energize solo tasks and make them feel more doable is to invite others to do them with you. Generally, your friends and family members love to be helpful and want to spend time with you, so it's a treat if they get to do both at once! Invite them to join you on a tree survey walk, to make seed bombs with you, or to help you cook for an upcoming block party. Doing this work with friends has the added benefit of you sharing your knowledge with others, and your loved ones might carry back what they've learned to their communities, expanding your impact without taxing your time.

Celebration

Don't forget to celebrate your milestones, big and small! Taking time to acknowledge the group's efforts makes people feel seen and valued in this work and makes it more likely that they'll stick around during the next challenge. Celebrations like a barbeque, a picnic at the park, or a potluck lunch at someone's apartment offer you a chance to get together without the seriousness of an agenda and can help mark the start of a new phase or project. Larry Yu, a climate activist, tells me that "when you're only together when you're fighting, you might associate your fellow travelers as fighters, rather than as neighbors and friends. It's neighbors and friends who sustain [us]."

When the repairs to the gas line were completed, Randi pulled together members of our coalition for a small celebratory moment. With a bottle of sparkling apple juice and a bouquet of flowers, the group stood at the site of the repaired leaks to collectively thank one another for the eighteen months of work it took to get the repairs made and trees replanted.

Block Parties

Although you may spend time identifying what needs to change, it's also important to spend time celebrating what's great about your neighborhood. People get discouraged if you only dwell on the negative about a place, so highlighting the benefits of a community is vital. Block parties are a great way to do that.

When I was a kid, every July our neighborhood blocked off the street to cars and held a gigantic, weekend-long block party, the centerpiece of which was an entire pig slow-roasted in the middle of the street. Kids would ride their bikes and jump rope while the old-timers and teens took turns playing DJ. Neighbors donated drinks, ice, food, equipment, and decorations, and for two full summer days and nights, the air filled with music, laughter, and conversation as we all connected and enjoyed one another's company. The neighbors who we danced and hula-hooped with were the same neighbors who I would see in the fall at the candlelight march against gun violence and the same neighbors who'd be there to help shovel out in a blizzard or lend their sump pump when the spring floods came. Your community's block parties don't need to be so big and ornate. A couple bags of chips and an upbeat playlist are really all it takes.

Creating an opportunity to get to know your community isn't

just great for keeping your social cup filled, it's also a great way to prepare for an emergency. The time to get to know your neighbors—including those who need help and those whom you can turn to for help—isn't during a crisis, it's right now. Block parties create a smooth, low-stress environment to learn more about the people around you. Stephanie Galaitsi, an environmental scientist, transportation advocate, and frequent block party host, is a huge fan of the gatherings for both the way they help us reenvision how to use public space and how they connect people. "When a climate catastrophe occurs, we will need our communities to support us," Galaitsi told me. "This has been emphasized with the recent disasters in Vermont and Lahaina [Hawaii]; throw a block party now so that if things go south, you know your neighbors." Knowing that you have neighbors to turn to in a crisis can lift your spirits and help you feel more connected to and invested in making change in your community.

Name Your Purpose

Brittney Cooper writes in her book *Eloquent Rage* that "joy arises from internal clarity about our purpose. . . . Maintaining the capacity for joy is critical to the struggle for justice."[1] One of the most powerful things you can do to stay invested for the long haul is to find your purpose for engaging in this work and return to it when things get tough. What calls *you* to do this work is deeply personal. Making progress that's in line with your purpose is a stabilizing force that allows us to prioritize the individual pleasure of what we've accomplished over the anxiety of what is left to do.

When I was growing up, I heard from so many adults in my life that I needed to work hard, get a career, and move out of my community. Years later, as a New York City public school teacher, my students' walk to school took them past scrap yards, dusty lots filled with household trash, and no trees to speak of. I told them the same thing I was told. Work hard, get a career, move on. Embarrassingly, it took me five years to realize what a horrifying thing that is to say to a child. Rooted in the painful myth of scrappy self-determinism, what we're really advising people to do is to leave their friends, their language, and their culture just for a shot at parks and dry streets, fresh air, and clean water. My purpose, or what calls me to do what I do, is rooted in the belief that everyone, not just those with enough resources, deserves a nice, safe, clean place to live. I can measure the progress against that purpose with every gas leak fixed, tree in the ground, and degree of cooling. Consider what calls you to engage in this work and what changes you'd like to see.

Thank Yourself

Finally, don't forget to turn that gratitude inward toward yourself. While there's no way to reverse the damage done to the planet, we can and must put in the work to keep our communities safer from the changing climate. You're one of the people who has decided to apply your time and energy to making a difference, and that's a big deal! Thank you. Each change you make to the built environment, each policy you advocate for, each friend you engage on the topic of the climate crisis brings us one step closer to creating a climate safe neighborhood.

Acknowledgments

I ANTICIPATED PUTTING A GOOD BIT OF TIME into writing this book. What I didn't anticipate is the incredible amount of community and financial support that carving out the time and energy to write requires. Behind the scenes, there's an impressive roster of kind and encouraging family and friends who have taken on extra domestic labor, endured my absences, and provided all manner of support—without them I wouldn't have started or completed this book.

Love and thanks to my partner, Cole, and to our daughter, who worked hard to make space in our life for me to research, think, and write. To the team of parents who modeled what it's like to come from a place of love in all that you do—Mom, Bubbie, Mal, and my aunt Catherine—thank you. To my warm and caring friends who believed in this book, and in me, before I did and showed up with food, silly tchotchkes, and kind words to smooth the way: Gisselle, Julian, Serena, Alison, Marilyn, Benazeer, Claire, Neela, Jossie, Julie, Mia, and Lucy—thank you, I hope this book is helpful.

Thank you to Randi Soltysiak, Bob Ackley, Jesse Clingan, and the members of our local chapter of Mothers Out Front for your determination, creativity, and belief that sometimes David *can* beat Goliath. The new trees are all planted and thriving, thanks to you!

For the last six years I've worked with Groundwork USA and the Groundwork network on issues of land use, climate adaptation, and policy change. My deepest learnings about community transformation have come from working with the dedicated organizers and residents who are putting in the hours, wearing out the soles of their shoes as they make tangible change across the United States. Thank you to the team of organizers and specialists I've had the joy of working so closely with and from whom I've learned so much; your thoughtful, values-driven leadership shows the world that change is already happening: Eric Andrade, Patrice Baker, Jasmin Barco, Abdirahman Buul, Leandro Castro, Cindy Chang, Damien DeBuhr, Alan Edwards, Riley Essert, John Evangelista, Celeste Gambino, Brigitte Griswold, Melissa Guevara, Kelsey Hawkins-Johnson, Pablo Herreros Cantis, Jeremy Hoffman, Matt Holmes, Oded Holzinger, Rob Jones, Young Kim, Lesly Melendez, Jackie Park-Albaum, Jonathan Phillips, Sophie Revis, Leslie Reynolds, Todd Reynolds, Eddie Rosa, Amelia Rose, Vivek Shandas, Kelly Shinn, Maura Valdez, Sam Villatoro, and Tan Yess.

Thank you to Jalisa Gilmore and John Valinch, from whom I've learned so much about so many things and with whom I've laughed about so many more.

Thank you to Dr. Jalonne White-Newsome, Yeou-Rong Jih, Kate O'Brien, and Minna Toloui for creating space to learn, feel, and synthesize what all this means; the biggest leaps in my understanding and inspiration have been a result of the CREWS convenings. Thanks and special appreciation to Abbie Dusseldorp, Lawrence Hoffman, and Stacey Moran, with whom I built, grew, and came to understand and articulate the early phases of the work presented in this book; I'm grateful for our partnership and friendship.

Thank you to Steve Burrington for your vision, guidance, support, and belief in me. Your mark is indelible, both upon me and upon all the communities you've championed.

Thank you to Island Press for the opportunity to pull these ideas together and the support you gave to make it happen. Thank you to Kathleen Lafferty, my copy editor. A giant thunderclap of thanks and appreciation to my editor, Stacy Eisenstark, for your grit, patience, and creativity in teaching me how to communicate through this long-form medium—I didn't know beans about it before I met you.

Notes

Chapter One

1. Richard Rothstein, *The Color of Law: A Forgotten History of How Our Government Segregated America* (New York: Liveright, 2017). I highly recommend reading Rothstein's *The Color of Law*. It's not an emotionally easy read, but it's one of the most important for understanding why we feel the echoes slavery and segregation so strongly today.

2. Hop online to the University of Virginia's Mapping Inequality project, which has digitized all known redlining maps. Check out your city or a city you're familiar with and note the similarities and differences between how certain neighborhoods were thought of in the 1930s and how they're thought of today. See Robert K. Nelson et al., "Mapping Inequality," *American Panorama*, ed. Robert K. Nelson and Edward L. Ayers, accessed September 19, 2023, https://dsl.richmond.edu/panorama/redlining/.

3. During World War II, Black residents from the South migrated to the shipyards in Richmond, California, for work. Within years, that small city ballooned to nearly 100,000 residents, setting off a housing crisis. The federal government intervened by funding the development of public and private housing. In the contracts with developers, the federal and local governments stipulated that homes intended for Black residents be built from lower-quality materials—think plywood instead of planks and tin roofs instead of shingles. The intent was to displace and demolish Black neighborhoods once the war was over. For more on this story, see Shirley Ann Wilson Moore's *To Place Our Deeds: The African American Community in Richmond, California, 1910–1963* (Berkeley: University of California Press, 2001).

4. Redlining Map of Richmond, Virginia, and Environs, 4/3/1937; Residential Security Maps, 1933–1939; Records of the Federal Home Loan Bank Board, Record Group 195; National Archives at College Park, College Park, MD.

5. Shaun Harper, "Bank Will Pay $31 Million after Discriminating against Black and Latino Communities," *Forbes*, January 13, 2023, https://www.forbes.com/sites/shaunharper/2023 /01/13/31-million-to-black-and-latino-communities-in-lar gest-ever-housing-discrimination-lawsuit/. While made unlawful, the practice of race-based housing discrimination is still alive and well. In 2023, the US Department of Justice reached a $31 million settlement with City National Bank, which was accused of housing discrimination. Bank of America and Trident Mortgage (a Berkshire Hathaway company), among other lending institutions, have been similarly sued and fined.

6. James Richardson et al., *Redlining and Neighborhood Health*

(Washington, DC: National Community Reinvestment Coalition, September 2020), https://ncrc.org/holc-health/.
7. James Baldwin, "Black English: A Dishonest Argument" (speech, Wayne State University, Detroit, MI, 1980).
8. Jeremy S. Hoffman, Vivek Shandas, and Nicholas Pendleton, "The Effects of Historical Housing Policies on Resident Exposure to Intra-Urban Heat: A Study of 108 US Urban Areas," *Climate* 8, no. 1:12, https://doi.org/10.3390/cli8010012.
9. Richardson et al., *Redlining and Neighborhood Health*.
10. Climate Central, *Hot Zones: Urban Heat Islands* (Princeton, NJ: Climate Central, 2021), 3, accessed September 19, 2023, https://www.climatecentral.org/climate-matters/urban-heat-islands.

Chapter Two

1. Andres Picon and Jerome Campbell, "Schools Cancel Classes or Dismiss Students Early during Heat Wave," *Boston Globe*, August 29, 2018, https://www.bostonglobe.com/metro/2018/08/29/schools-cancel-classes-dismiss-students-early-during-heat-wave/eXpyG5KE7TwJWTwEUeg7kL/story.html.
2. Kyle Stokes, "The Extreme Heat in California Is Causing Disruptions in the State's Classrooms," interview by Alisa Chang, *All Things Considered*, NPR, September 7, 2022, transcript, https://www.npr.org/2022/09/07/1121599322/the-extreme-heat-in-california-is-causing-disruptions-in-the-states-classrooms; Kathiann M. Kowalski, "Ohio Schools Focus on Air Conditioning as They Feel the Heat from Climate Change," *Energy News Network*, August 30, 2022, https://energynews.us/2022/08/30/ohio-schools-focus-on-air-conditioning-as-they-feel-the-heat-from-climate-change.
3. Terri Adams-Fuller, "Extreme Heat Is Deadlier than Hurricanes,

Floods, and Tornadoes Combined," *Scientific American*, July 1, 2023, https://www.scientificamerican.com/article/extreme -heat-is-deadlier-than-hurricanes-floods-and-tornadoes -combined.

4. In 2021, the city of Phoenix, Arizona, established one of the country's first Offices of Heat Response and Mitigation. We'll talk about systems-level change later, but this is a good addition to local government to keep an eye on. Such a dedicated office gives the city of Phoenix a branch of government that's laser-focused on keeping people alive and well during heat waves. Who in your municipality is responsible for public welfare during extreme heat events?

5. Dave Roos, "Native Americans Used Fire to Protect and Cultivate Land," History, updated August 11, 2023, https://www .history.com/news/native-american-wildfires.

6. Kat Kerlin, "California's 2020 Wildfire Season," University of California, Davis, news, May 4, 2022, https://www.ucda vis.edu/climate/news/californias-2020-wildfire-season-num bers.

7. US Fire Administration, "What Is the WUI?," accessed September 14, 2023, https://www.usfa.fema.gov/wui/what-is-the -wui.html.

8. Aatish Bhatia, Josh Katz, and Margot Sanger-Katz, "Just How Bad Was the Pollution in New York?," *New York Times*, updated June 9, 2023, https://www.nytimes.com/interactive/20 23/06/08/upshot/new-york-city-smoke.html.

9. US Environmental Protection Agency, "Why Wildfire Smoke Is a Health Concern," accessed September 14, 2023, https:// www.epa.gov/wildfire-smoke-course/why-wildfire-smoke -health-concern.

10. Tony Briscoe, "Pollution from California's 2020 Wildfires Likely Offset Decades of Air Quality Gains," *Los Angeles Times*, June 17, 2022, https://www.latimes.com/environment /story/2022-06-17/2020-california-wildfires-offset-decades -of-air-quality-gains.

11. Katharine Hayhoe et al., "Our Changing Climate," in *Impacts, Risks, and Adaptation in the United States: Fourth National Climate Assessment*, vol. 2 (Washington, DC: US Global Change Research Program, 2018), 72–144, https://nca2018 .globalchange.gov/chapter/2/.

12. Catherine Coleman Flowers, *Waste: One Woman's Fight Against America's Dirty Secret* (New York: New Press, 2020), 128–34.

13. If you have an asphalt or rubber roof, don't use rain barrel water to irrigate edible herbs or leafy greens because there's a chance that chemical runoff from the roof will end up absorbed into the leaves of your basil and collards.

14. Massachusetts Water Resource Authority, "A History of the Sewer System," accessed September 14, 2023, https://www .mwra.com/03sewer/html/sewhist.htm.

15. Richmond, Virginia; Richmond, California; Denver, Colorado; Pawtucket and Central Falls, Rhode Island; Elizabeth, New Jersey; Yonkers, New York; Cincinnati, Ohio; San Diego, California; New Orleans, Louisiana; Fall River, New Bedford, Lawrence, and Somerville, Massachusetts; Milwaukee, Wisconsin; Kansas City, Kansas.

16. Combined sewer systems collect rainwater and domestic, industrial, and commercial sewage in the same pipe. Usually this method is fine, and the mixed water makes its way to the water treatment plant for processing. During rainstorms, however, the system can be overwhelmed with too much water, and

the system can experience a combined sewer overflow where the system discharges water, sewage, and industrial waste into nearby bodies of water or into city streets. These discharges are gross and extremely expensive and complex for cities to fix.

17. Emma Silvers, "You Can Adopt a Drain in San Francisco— With Naming Rights Included," KQED, January 5, 2023, https://www.kqed.org/arts/13923319/you-can-adopt-a-drain -in-san-francisco-with-naming-rights-included.

18. US Environmental Protection Agency, "Climate Change and Social Vulnerability in the United States: A Focus on Six Impacts," EPA 430-R-21_003, 2021, www.epa.gov/cira/social -vulnerability-report, 76.

19. US Environmental Protection Agency, "Climate Change and Social Vulnerability," 40.

Chapter Three

1. Jon Epps, "The Advancement of Asphalt Pavements Over the Last 50 Years," *Asphalt Magazine* 36, no. 2 (Summer 2021): 28–39. Yes! I know! I was also surprised to see that there's an asphalt magazine!

2. Linda Poon, "The Quest to Make Composting as Simple as Trash Collection," *Bloomberg CityLab*, October 14, 2021, https://www.bloomberg.com/news/articles/2021-10-14/ame rica-s-uphill-trudge-to-universal-curbside-composting.

3. Peter Wohlleben, *The Hidden Life of Trees: What They Feel, How They Communicate—Discoveries from a Secret World*, trans. Jane Billinghurst (Vancouver: Greystone Books, 2016). If you want to have your mind absolutely blown, pick up *The Hidden Life of Trees*. It's an extremely short, easy read about the unique abilities of trees.

4. David J. Nowak and Eric J. Greenfield, "Declining Urban and

Community Tree Cover in the United States," *Urban Forestry and Urban Greening* 32, (May 2018): 32–55, https://doi.org/10.1016/j.ufug.2018.03.006.

5. Cleveland Tree Coalition, "The Cleveland Tree Plan," accessed September 15, 2023, http://www.clevelandtrees.org/cleveland-tree-plan/.

6. Fried ginkgo nuts are delicious! Those who aren't used to the berries that contain them may be bothered by their strong smell, however.

7. Benjamin Storrow, "Methane Leaks Erase Some of the Climate Benefits of Natural Gas," *Scientific American*, May 5, 2020, https://www.scientificamerican.com/article/methane-leaks-erase-some-of-the-climate-benefits-of-natural-gas/

8. Maryann R. Sargent et al., "Majority of US Urban Natural Gas Emissions Unaccounted for in Inventories," *Proceedings of the National Academy of Sciences* 118, no. 44 (2021), https://doi.org/10.1073/pnas.2105804118.

9. Urban Forests, "Method," accessed September 15, 2023, https://urban-forests.com/miyawaki-method/.

10. Sarah Owens, "Could Microforests Help Keep Bradenton and Sarasota Cool? What Experts Say," *Bradenton Herald*, July 3, 2023, https://www.bradenton.com/news/local/article276911953.html.

11. Hannah Lewis, *Mini-Forest Revolution: Using the Miyawaki Method to Rapidly Rewild the World* (White River Junction, VT: Chelsea Green, 2022). This book is a solid primer on microforests.

12. If you want to get an urban forester's eye to twitch, bring up the emerald ash borer (EAB). At time of writing, this insect has invaded thirty states and caused the death of tens of millions of ash and fringe trees. The EAB lays eggs under the bark

of ash trees, and once hatched, the larvae feast on the tissues that transport water and sugar throughout the trunk, starving the tree in as little as a year. If you see an ash tree covered in woodpeckers (who are trying to feast on the larvae), with wilted, yellow leaves or D-shaped holes in the trunk, give your urban forester a call. Also, and this is important, EABs love to travel via firewood, so if you're into camping or hosting backyard firepits, use and burn only local wood to prevent destructive hitchhikers.

Chapter Four

1. Pirkei Avot 1:14.
2. Theodore Roosevelt, Address of President Roosevelt at Grand Canyon, Arizona, May 6, 1903, Theodore Roosevelt Papers, Library of Congress Manuscript Division, https://www.theodorerooseveltcenter.org/Research/Digital-Library/Record?libID=o289796, Theodore Roosevelt Digital Library, Dickinson State University.
3. Char Miller, "Play, Work, and Politics: The Remarkable Partnership of Theodore Roosevelt and Gifford Pinchot," in *Theodore Roosevelt, Naturalist in the Arena*, ed. Char Miller and Clay S. Jenkinson (Lincoln: University of Nebraska Press, 2020), 115.
4. For another look at the racist origins and actions of the conservation movement, see Jedediah Purdy, "Environmentalism's Racist History," *New Yorker*, August 13, 2015, https://www.newyorker.com/news/news-desk/environmentalisms-racist-history.
5. Sarah Kuta, "Why Ten Billion Snow Crabs Disappeared Off the Coast of Alaska," *Smithsonian*, October 20, 2023, https://www.smithsonianmag.com/smart-news/why-10-billion-snow-crabs-disappeared-off-the-coast-of-alaska-180983112/.

6. Marshall Ganz, a Freedom Summer alum, is most well known for his time spent in agricultural labor organizing alongside Cesar Chavez in the 1960s and 1970s.

7. Channelization is the source of a lot of drama and tension in the planning and engineering world. It's effectively using civil engineering methods to try to control flooding near moving bodies of water. Sometimes that means straightening a winding river and sometimes that means adding concrete barriers to the shore of a stream, but the ultimate goal is to try to control flooding with human-made interventions. Feelings these days are mixed on channelization, with many advocates arguing that historical human-made interventions are ineffective, especially in the face of increased precipitation and record flooding. Instead, they argue, we need to better understand and mimic the natural environment, which may mean reframing wetland features along a river (such as trees, plants, decaying logs, and marshy areas) as integral flood prevention infrastructure instead of as a barrier to controlling the flow of water. I'm not an expert in this specific area, but I will say that if waste is ending up in your home from a nearby body of water, there's an infrastructure problem afoot one way or the other that needs to be dealt with.

Chapter Five

1. Not every municipality has an urban forester or an urban forestry committee. Use an online search engine and search terms such as "city, state urban forestry committee," "city, state urban tree advisory committee," "city, state arborist," and "city, state urban forestry" to see if there's one where you live. Example: "Tallahassee, Florida, urban forestry committee."

2. Richard Weissbourd et al., *Loneliness in America: How the Pandemic Has Deepened an Epidemic of Loneliness and What*

We Can Do about It (Cambridge, MA: Making Caring Common Project, Harvard Graduate School of Education, 2021), https://mcc.gse.harvard.edu/reports/loneliness-in-america.

Chapter Six

1. Most large municipalities allow you to call 311 from your cell phone or landline and request action on nonemergency issues such as potholes, rat sightings, or needles on the sidewalk needing cleanup.
2. You might also have something called a "councilor at large," who is a member of the body that is elected by and represents the entire city instead of a geographically defined district or "ward."
3. Who Votes for Mayor?, "Low Voter Turnout Is a Problem in Cities across the Country," accessed September 15, 2023, http://whovotesformayor.org/.
4. Felix Kapoor and Alice Liu, "Unclogging Climate Injustices Requires Persistent Community Action," *Next City*, August 3, 2023, https://nextcity.org/urbanist-news/unclogging-climate-injustices-requires-persistent-community-action.
5. In some smaller communities, the council is responsible for drafting and approving the budget.
6. Metropolitan Government of Nashville and Davidson County, "Participatory Budgeting," accessed September 15, 2023, https://www.nashville.gov/departments/mayor/participatory-budgeting.

Chapter Seven

1. HEET, "The Gas Leaks Map," accessed September 15, 2023, https://heet.org/gas-leaks/gas-leak-maps/.
2. GIS allows you to take georeferenced data and turn it into maps and images to be viewed and analyzed.

3. National Integrated Heat Health Information System, "Mapping Campaigns," accessed September 15, 2023, https://www.heat.gov/pages/mapping-campaigns. At time of writing, the Heat Watch campaigns have mapped more than sixty US municipalities.

4. Green Team is a paid environmental justice program for youth ages thirteen through eighteen.

5. To be clear, race does, and has always, mattered in the US context, and it certainly matters in issues of environmental justice. However, in dominant American culture, we still struggle to find common language around race. I've found that the use of maps to visualize disparities in how people experience the climate crisis helps open the door to more fruitful and collaborative conversations around environmental and racial justice.

6. Promotoras are Hispanic community members who are trained to provide basic health information and education within Spanish-speaking communities.

7. Association of Science and Technology Centers, "Introduction to Community Science," accessed September 15, 2023, https://communityscience.astc.org/overview/. There are a number of great online primers for how to conduct effective community science initiatives. This is a great place to get started.

8. US Environmental Protection Agency, Office of Research and Development, *Black Carbon Research and Future Strategies*, Washington, DC: EPA, 2011, https://www.epa.gov/sites/default/files/2013-12/documents/black-carbon-fact-sheet_0.pdf.

9. Rutgers University, Center for Environmental Exposures and Disease, "Countdown to Cleaner Air: Street Scientists and the Fight for First Street," YouTube video, 8:22, 2018, https://youtu.be/uM2gjytmzeo. To learn more about this community science initiative, check out this wonderful video profiling the work and its impacts.

10. United States Census Bureau, "American Community Survey (ACS)," last modified September 7, 2023, https://www.census .gov/programs-surveys/acs.

11. Casey Mullen et al., "Exploring the Distributional Environ-mental Justice Implications of an Air Quality Monitoring Network in Los Angeles County," *Environmental Research* 206 (April 2022): 112612, https://doi.org/10.1016/j.envres.2021 .112612.

Chapter Eight

1. Canbing Li et al., "Hidden Benefits of Electric Vehicles for Addressing Climate Change," *Scientific Reports* 5 (2015): 9213, https://doi.org/10.1038/srep09213. This study reveals the contribution to the urban heat island effect made by con-ventional cars with combustion engines.

2. You can review the text of the ordinance at Cambridgema.gov, "Cycling Safety Ordinance," last modified August 23, 2023, https://www.cambridgema.gov/streetsandtransportation/po liciesordinancesandplans/cyclingsafetyordinance.

3. LouisvilleKy.gov, "Park Improvement Projects and Master Plans," accessed September 18, 2023, https://louisvilleky.gov /government/parks/park-improvement-projects-and-master -plans.

4. Chicago.gov, "Sustainable Urban Infrastructure Guidelines," accessed September 18, 2023, https://www.chicago.gov/city /en/depts/cdot/supp_info/sustainable_urbaninfrastucture guidelines.html.

5. US Environmental Protection Agency, "Cool Roofs," *Reducing Urban Heat Islands: Compendium of Strategies*, draft, 2008: 4, https://www.epa.gov/heat-islands/heat-island-compendium.

6. Houston Permitting Center, "Building Code Enforcement:

Roof Repair and Cool Roof Guidelines," last modified October 16, 2019, https://www.houstonpermittingcenter.org/media/2041/download.

7. Richard Florida, "Why Greenway Parks Cause Greater Gentrification," *Bloomberg CityLab*, October 10, 2019, https://www.bloomberg.com/news/articles/2019-10-10/why-greenway-parks-cause-greater-gentrification; Isabelle Anguelovski et al. "Green Gentrification in European and North American Cities," *Nature Communications* 13, 3816 (2022), https://doi.org/10.1038/s41467-022-31572-1.

8. Matthew Goldstein, "Where a Little Mortgage Goes a Long Way," *New York Times*, August 2, 2020, https://www.nytimes.com/2020/08/02/business/mortgages-affordable-housing.html.

9. "Historically Black Neighborhoods Need to Be #PolicyProtected!," Historically Black Neighborhood Assembly, accessed September 18, 2023, https://www.hbnassembly.org/hbno.

Conclusion

1. Brittney Cooper, *Eloquent Rage: A Black Feminist Discovers Her Superpower* (New York: St. Martin's, 2018), 274.

Bibliography

Adams-Fuller, Terri. "Extreme Heat Is Deadlier than Hurricanes, Floods, and Tornadoes Combined." *Scientific American*, July 1, 2023. https://www.scientificamerican.com/article/extreme-heat -is-deadlier-than-hurricanes-floods-and-tornadoes-combined.

Anguelovski, Isabelle, James J. T. Connolly, Helen Cole, Melissa Garcia-Lamarca, Margarita Triguero-Mas, Francesc Baró, Nicholas Martin, et al. "Green Gentrification in European and North American Cities." *Nature Communications* 13, 3816 (2022). https://doi.org/10.1038/s41467-022-31572-1.

Association of Science and Technology Centers. "Introduction to Community Science." Accessed September 15, 2023. https://communityscience.astc.org/overview/.

Baldwin, James. "Black English: A Dishonest Argument." Speech. Wayne State University, Detroit, MI, 1980.

Bhatia, Aatish, Josh Katz, and Margot Sanger-Katz. "Just How Bad Was the Pollution in New York?" *New York Times*, updated June 9, 2023. https://www.nytimes.com/interactive/2023/06 /08/upshot/new-york-city-smoke.html.

Briscoe, Tony. "Pollution from California's 2020 Wildfires Likely Offset Decades of Air Quality Gains." *Los Angeles Times*, June 17, 2022. https://www.latimes.com/environment/story/2022 -06-17/2020-california-wildfires-offset-decades-of-air-quality -gains.

Cambridgema.gov. "Cycling Safety Ordinance." Last modified August 23, 2023. https://www.cambridgema.gov/streetsandtrans portation/policiesordinancesandplans/cyclingsafetyordinance.

CAPA Strategies. "Heat Watch." Accessed September 18, 2023. https://www.capastrategies.com/heat-watch.

Chicago.gov. "Sustainable Urban Infrastructure Guidelines." Accessed September 18, 2023. https://www.chicago.gov/city/en /depts/cdot/supp_info/sustainable_urbaninfrastuctureguide lines.html.

Cleveland Tree Coalition. "The Cleveland Tree Plan." Accessed September 15, 2023. http://www.clevelandtrees.org/cleveland -tree-plan/.

Climate Central. *Hot Zones: Urban Heat Islands*. Princeton, NJ: Climate Central, 2021. Accessed September 19, 2023. https:// www.climatecentral.org/climate-matters/urban-heat-islands.

Cooper, Brittney. *Eloquent Rage: A Black Feminist Discovers Her Superpower*. New York: St. Martin's, 2018.

Epps, Jon. "The Advancement of Asphalt Pavements Over the Last 50 Years." *Asphalt Magazine* 36, no. 2 (Summer 2021): 28–39.

Florida, Richard. "Why Greenway Parks Cause Greater Gentrification." *Bloomberg CityLab*, October 10, 2019. https://www.bl oomberg.com/news/articles/2019-10-10/why-greenway-parks -cause-greater-gentrification.

Flowers, Catherine Coleman, *Waste: One Woman's Fight Against America's Dirty Secret*. New York: New Press, 2020.

Goldstein, Matthew. "Where a Little Mortgage Goes a Long Way."

New York Times, August 2, 2020. https://www.nytimes.com/20
20/08/02/business/mortgages-affordable-housing.html.

Groundwork USA. "Climate Safe Neighborhoods." Accessed September 19, 2023. https://groundworkusa.org/what-we-do/climate-safe-neighborhoods/.

Harper, Shaun. "Bank Will Pay $31 Million after Discriminating against Black and Latino Communities." *Forbes*, January 13, 2023. https://www.forbes.com/sites/shaunharper/2023/01/13/31-million-to-black-and-latino-communities-in-largest-ever-housing-discrimination-lawsuit/.

Hayhoe, Katharine, Donald J. Wuebbles, David R. Easterling, David W. Fahey, Sarah Doherty, James P. Kossin, William V. Sweet, Russell S. Vose, and Michael F. Wehner. "Our Changing Climate." *Impacts, Risks, and Adaptation in the United States: Fourth National Climate Assessment*, vol. 2, chap. 2. Washington, DC: US Global Change Research Program, 2018: 72–144. doi:10.7930/NCA4.2018.CH2.

HEET. "The Gas Leaks Map." Accessed September 15, 2023. https://heet.org/gas-leaks/gas-leak-maps/.

Historically Black Neighborhood Assembly. "Historically Black Neighborhoods Need to Be #PolicyProtected!" Accessed September 18, 2023. https://www.hbnassembly.org/hbno.

Hoffman, Jeremy S., Vivek Shandas, and Nicholas Pendleton. "The Effects of Historical Housing Policies on Resident Exposure to Intra-Urban Heat: A Study of 108 US Urban Areas." *Climate* 8, no. 1:12. https://doi.org/10.3390/cli8010012.

Houston Permitting Center. "Building Code Enforcement: Roof Repair and Cool Roof Guidelines." Last modified October 16, 2019. https://www.houstonpermittingcenter.org/media/2041/download.

Kapoor, Felix, and Alice Liu. "Unclogging Climate Injustices

Requires Persistent Community Action." *Next City*, August 3, 2023. https://nextcity.org/urbanist-news/unclogging-climate -injustices-requires-persistent-community-action.

Kerlin, Kat. "California's 2020 Wildfire Season." University of California, Davis, News, May 4, 2022. https://www.ucdavis .edu/climate/news/californias-2020-wildfire-season-numbers.

Kowalski, Kathiann M. "Ohio Schools Focus on Air Condition- ing as They Feel the Heat from Climate Change." *Energy News Network*, August 30, 2022. https://energynews.us/2022/08/30 /ohio-schools-focus-on-air-conditioning-as-they-feel-the-heat -from-climate-change.

Kuta, Sarah. "Why Ten Billion Snow Crabs Disappeared Off the Coast of Alaska" *Smithsonian*, October 20, 2023. https://www .smithsonianmag.com/smart-news/why-10-billion-snow-crabs -disappeared-off-the-coast-of-alaska-180983112/.

Lewis, Hannah. *Mini-Forest Revolution: Using the Miyawaki Method to Rapidly Rewild the World*. White River Junction, VT: Chelsea Green, 2022.

LouisvilleKy.gov. "Park Improvement Projects and Master Plans." Accessed September 18, 2023. https://louisvilleky.gov/govern ment/parks/park-improvement-projects-and-master-plans.

Li, Canbing, Yijia Cao, Mi Zhang, Jianhui Wang, Jianguo Liu, Haiqing Shi, and Yinghui Geng. "Hidden Benefits of Electric Vehicles for Addressing Climate Change." *Scientific Reports* 5 (2015): 9213. https://doi.org/10.1038/srep09213.

Massachusetts Water Resource Authority. "A History of the Sewer System." Accessed September 14, 2023. https://www.mwra .com/03sewer/html/sewhist.htm.

Metropolitan Government of Nashville and Davidson County. "Participatory Budgeting." Accessed September 15, 2023. https://www.nashville.gov/departments/mayor/participatory -budgeting.

Miller, Char. "Play, Work, and Politics: The Remarkable Partnership of Theodore Roosevelt and Gifford Pinchot." In *Theodore Roosevelt, Naturalist in the Arena*, edited by Char Miller and Clay S. Jenkinson, 101–20. Lincoln: University of Nebraska Press, 2020.

Moore, Shirley Ann Wilson. *To Place Our Deeds: The African American Community in Richmond, California, 1910–1963.* Berkeley: University of California Press, 2001.

Mullen, Casey, Aaron Flores, Sara Grineski, and Timothy Collins. "Exploring the Distributional Environmental Justice Implications of an Air Quality Monitoring Network in Los Angeles County." *Environmental Research* 206 (April 2022): 112612. https://doi.org/10.1016/j.envres.2021.112612.

National Integrated Heat Health Information System. "Mapping Campaigns." Accessed September 15, 2023. https://www.heat.gov/pages/mapping-campaigns.

Nelson, Robert K., LaDale Winling, Richard Marciano, Nathan Connolly, et al. "Mapping Inequality." Accessed September 19, 2023. https://dsl.richmond.edu/panorama/redlining/.

Nowak, David J., and Eric J. Greenfield. "Declining Urban and Community Tree Cover in the United States." *Urban Forestry and Urban Greening* 32 (May 2018): 32–55. https://doi.org/10.1016/j.ufug.2018.03.006.

Owens, Sarah. "Could Microforests Help Keep Bradenton and Sarasota Cool? What Experts Say." *Bradenton Herald*, July 3, 2023. https://www.bradenton.com/news/local/article276911953.html.

Picon, Andres, and Jerome Campbell. "Schools Cancel Classes or Dismiss Students Early during Heat Wave." *Boston Globe*, August 29, 2018. https://www.bostonglobe.com/metro/2018/08/29/schools-cancel-classes-dismiss-students-early-during-heat-wave/eXpyG5KE7TwJWTwEUeg7kL/story.html.

Poon, Linda. "The Quest to Make Composting as Simple as Trash Collection." *Bloomberg CityLab*, October 14, 2021. https://www.bloomberg.com/news/articles/2021-10-14/america-s-uphill-trudge-to-universal-curbside-composting.

Purdy, Jedediah. "Environmentalism's Racist History." *New Yorker*, August 13, 2015. https://www.newyorker.com/news/news-desk/environmentalisms-racist-history.

Richardson, James, Bruce C. Mitchell, Helen C. S. Meier, Emily Lynch, and Jad Edlebi. *Redlining and Neighborhood Health*. Washington, DC: National Community Reinvestment Coalition, 2020. https://ncrc.org/holc-health/.

Roos, Dave. "Native Americans Used Fire to Protect and Cultivate Land." *History*, A&E Television Networks, updated August 11, 2023. https://www.history.com/news/native-american-wild fires.

Roosevelt, Theodore. Address of President Roosevelt at Grand Canyon, Arizona, May 6, 1903. Theodore Roosevelt Papers. Library of Congress Manuscript Division, https://www.theodorerooseveltcenter.org/Research/Digital-Library/Record?libID=o289796, Theodore Roosevelt Digital Library. Dickinson State University.

Rothstein, Richard. *The Color of Law: A Forgotten History of How Our Government Segregated America*. New York: Liveright, 2017.

Rutgers University, Center for Environmental Exposures and Disease. "Countdown to Cleaner Air: Street Scientists and the Fight for First Street." 2018. YouTube video, 8:22. https://youtu.be/uM2gjytmzeo.

Sargent, Maryann R., Cody Floerchinger, Kathryn McKain, John Budney, Elaine W. Gottlieb, Lucy R. Hutyra, Joseph Rudek, and Steven C. Wofsy. "Majority of US Urban Natural Gas Emissions Unaccounted for in Inventories." *Proceedings of the*

National Academy of Sciences 118, no. 44 (2021). https://doi.org /10.1073/pnas.2105804118.

Silvers, Emma. "You Can Adopt a Drain in San Francisco—With Naming Rights Included." KQED, January 5, 2023. https:// www.kqed.org/arts/13923319/you-can-adopt-a-drain-in-san -francisco-with-naming-rights-included.

Stokes, Kyle. "The Extreme Heat in California Is Causing Disruptions in the State's Classrooms." Interview by Alisa Chang, *All Things Considered*, NPR, September 7, 2022. Transcript. https:// www.npr.org/2022/09/07/1121599322/the-extreme-heat-in -california-is-causing-disruptions-in-the-states-classrooms.

Storrow, Benjamin. "Methane Leaks Erase Some of the Climate Benefits of Natural Gas." *Scientific American*, May 5, 2020. https://www.scientificamerican.com/article/methane-leaks-era se-some-of-the-climate-benefits-of-natural-gas/.

Urban Forests. "Method." Accessed September 15, 2023. https:// urban-forests.com/miyawaki-method/.

US Census Bureau. "American Community Survey (ACS)." Last modified September 7, 2023. https://www.census.gov/programs -surveys/acs.

US Environmental Protection Agency. Office of Research and Development. *Black Carbon Research and Future Strategies*. Washington, DC: EPA, 2011. https://www.epa.gov/sites/default/files /2013-12/documents/black-carbon-fact-sheet_0.pdf.

US Environmental Protection Agency. "Climate Change and Social Vulnerability in the United States: A Focus on Six Impacts." EPA 430-R-21_003, 2021. www.epa.gov/cira/social-vulnerabi lity-report.

US Environmental Protection Agency. "Cool Roofs." *Reducing Urban Heat Islands: Compendium of Strategies*. Draft. 2008: 4. https://www.epa.gov/heat-islands/heat-island-compendium.

US Environmental Protection Agency. "Why Wildfire Smoke Is a Health Concern." Accessed September 14, 2023. https://www.epa.gov/wildfire-smoke-course/why-wildfire-smoke-health-concern.

US Fire Administration. "What Is the WUI?" Accessed September 14, 2023. https://www.usfa.fema.gov/wui/what-is-the-wui.html.

Weissbourd, Richard, Milena Batanova, Virginia Lovison, and Eric Torres. *Loneliness in America: How the Pandemic Has Deepened an Epidemic of Loneliness and What We Can Do about It.* Cambridge, MA: Making Caring Common Project, Harvard Graduate School of Education, 2021. https://mcc.gse.harvard.edu/reports/loneliness-in-america.

Who Votes for Mayor? "Low Voter Turnout Is a Problem in Cities across the Country." Accessed September 15, 2023. http://whovotesformayor.org/.

Wohlleben, Peter. *The Hidden Life of Trees: What They Feel, How They Communicate—Discoveries from a Secret World.* Translated by Jane Billinghurst. Vancouver: Greystone Books, 2016.

About the Author

Cate Mingoya-LaFortune is a people-centered climate adaptation planner, community organizer, educator, parent, and cautious optimist. Raised in an environmental justice neighborhood, she is committed to furthering a future where all people live in clean, thriving communities. She received a BA in biology from Reed College, a master of science education from CUNY Lehman, and a master of city planning from the Massachusetts Institute of Technology. She lives with her family and community in New England.